DAVID MURRELL FCA

Why Being A
WORLDWIDE ACCOUNTANT
Can Be So Exciting

novum pro

© 2025 novum publishing gmbh
Rathausgasse 73, A-7311 Neckenmarkt
office@novum-publishing.co.uk

ISBN 978-3-7116-0471-2
Editing: Samantha Acker
Cover photos: David Murrell FCA;
Viktoria Protsak I Dreamstime.com
Cover design, layout & typesetting:
novum publishing

www.novum-publishing.co.uk

All rights of distribution, including via film, radio, and television, photomechanical reproduction, audio storage media, electronic data storage media, and the reprinting of portions of text, are reserved.

Printed in the European Union on environmentally friendly, chlorine- and acid-free paper.

Contents

Introduction	7
Schooling and Early Working Years in Somerset	10
Early Years, Living in London	14
Early Years, Working for KPMG in London	17
Working for Banks	19
Working for Television Companies	22
Working for Film Companies	28
Acting as Receiver and Liquidator in the UK	31
Unusual and Unique Overseas Assignments	34
Working for Newspapers	47
Working for UK Radio Companies	49
Working with Chris Wright CBE, Sir George Martin and The Chrysalis Group	51
Working with Sir Richard Branson and The Virgin Group of Companies	53
Joining and Working with Film, Television and Radio Trade Organisations	55
Working For and With Significant Charities	58
Working Personally with Royalty	64
Working on Live Pop Tours	67
Leasing Hundreds of Cars	69
Worldwide Marketing of a Leading Professional Services Firm	71
Product Placement and Advertising Professional Firm	75
Playing Golf Worldwide	77
Television Appearances and the Media	88
Being an Expert Witness in Court Cases	93
Keeping in Touch with Former Employees (Sometimes Called Alumni)	95
Private London Members and Social Clubs	97

Opening Bars and Restaurants	99
Owning Racehorses	101
Significant Auction and Raffles Prizes	106
Sport Other than Golf	108
Long-Distance Car-Trialling and Owning Unusual Cars	112
Timeshare Ownerships in United States and in England (Some Good, Others Not So Much)	115
Life as a Head-Hunter	118
Working for Property Businesses	120
Mentoring Young Chartered Accountants' Careers	124
Index	126

Introduction

At various functions, people often inquire about an individual's occupation, background and achievements. When the answer is 'a chartered accountant', there often follows something approaching a yawn and a natural assumption by the inquirer that the person might be quite good at adding numbers.

They imagine that, he or she, as it is with business bookkeepers, would sit at the same desk in his or her permanent office for five days between 9 am and 5.30 pm every Monday through Friday, except for their annual holiday. This would involve adding numbers whilst preparing accounts and tax computations for small businesses. He or she may need to do some overtime and is normally allowed a normal number of weeks for holiday each year.

The above is often the case for bookkeepers in small firms of chartered accountants and business advisors, just as it was for David, who, at fifteen years of age, started a five-year training contract with a firm in Minehead in Somerset in the South West of England. He had obtained the sufficient O'level passing grades so he was allowed to work there.

This office dealt solely with a variety of local businesses for tax-payable calculation purposes and preparing accounts for lodgement at Companies House, if the business was a limited company. After the mandatory training of five years (now less than that) dealing with numerous different types of local businesses, he passed all the several examinations to become a Chartered Accountant at 21 years of age.

Very soon after, he successfully applied to and joined the London office of Peat, Marwick, Mitchell & Co. (now KPMG), one of the then-Big-Eight firms in London. This was with the intention to gain experience in numerous financial services dealing with much larger businesses. This would involve dealing with audits, tax compliance and advice, investigations and insolvencies and acquisitions often on a multinational scale.

The intention was that he would then return to take up a promised partnership in Minehead. However, David earned several promotions in a very short time in London and subsequently achieved two very senior different positions at the same time on the UK, European and Worldwide Boards of what became KPMG, one of the Big Four (formerly Big Eight before mergers) worldwide accounting and consulting firms.

At KPMG, there was only ever office space and desks for less than a quarter of their personnel as the work was usually carried out mainly at clients' premises where the management and the financial records were located. Sometimes, they were outside the accountant's home locality and sometimes outside the United Kingdom.

When it is mentioned that you have worked on a multitude of one-offs or more assignments of audits, financial advisory, tax and insolvencies and some financial assignments in nearly thirty countries in the world, including for some months each in some unusual countries, like Japan, Dubai, Kuwait, Saudi Arabia, Sudan, Hong Kong and the United States, as well as many countries in Europe, there is often an increasingly look of incredibility. This gets worse when you state that you have enjoyed holidays in another twenty countries, including Antarctica and the Arctic.

It also raises eyebrows when, in response to the question of, 'Have you ever worked with anybody famous?' you mention, amongst many others, you have entertained H.M. The King, the late H.M. The Queen, the late Duke of Edinburgh, the Duchess of Cornwall, the Princess Royal and Prince Edward and sat next to several of them at charitable and business events, this seems to border on further incredulity. This gets even more remarkable when you have assisted a senior Government minister on a project to enhance funding for the UK's film industry.

David has enjoyed working personally with numerous media and entertainment business icons, like Sir Richard Branson,

Chris Wright CBE, Sir George Martin and Sir Christopher Bland; this garners further astonishment and questions, like, 'What are they like to deal with?' He has also worked free of charge for several well-known charities, like being the receipts collector for Comic Relief, president and a committee member of the Film and Television Charity (formerly the Cinema and Television Benevolent Fund) and a member of the Variety Golf charity and others.

When it comes to sport, further amazement follows when it gets mentioned that you played golf in the Pro-Am Tournaments in Continental Europe on the European Golf Tour three times in the 1990s, and, later, as the worldwide head of marketing at KPMG, personally organised the corporate sponsorship for KPMG of well-known professional golfers on the European Tour and the European Seniors Tour. This led to the signing of KPMG's sponsorship of some of the most popular professional golfers in the world, including Phil Mickelson, which still existed until very recently.

David was at Wembley in 1966 on the day that England won the football World Cup for the first and only time, and this also sparks incredulity again as with being an expert witness in a media court case. The same reaction occurs when it is mentioned you worked on the Rolling Stones and Pink Floyd tours and that you owned racehorses.

This is the true story of a UK Country Boy accountant, who was, for more than three decades, one of the best known financial professionals operating in the United Kingdom, European and worldwide film, television, radio and other media and entertainment industries, featuring royalty, famous businesses and businesspeople, charities and sportsmen. Simultaneously, for a while, he was KPMG's head of the UK, European and worldwide information, communications, media and entertainment practices, and head of KPMG's UK, European and worldwide marketing.

It just shows Why Being A Worldwide Accountant Can Be So Exciting.

Schooling and Early Working Years in Somerset

For five years, starting from age five, I attended the local school in Minehead, Somerset, and somehow or other, five years later managed to pass the entrance examination to Taunton (Public) School in Somerset. This was 25 miles away at one of the three private schools in that town. Every school day, this necessitated a 25-mile, each way, steam-train journey between Minehead and Taunton, leaving home at 7 am and returning in the late afternoon.

With the loss of my father's father very early on in his life leading to his mother and family being impoverished, my father managed to secure a scholarship to Taunton School, one of the three public schools in that town. My two brothers were seven and nine years older than me, with the gap being attributable to my father being posted to West Africa during the Second World War. Both of my brothers had attempted unsuccessfully to obtain the very small number of available scholarships, which would have provided them with free schooling at Taunton School starting from age 11, so my father had to pay the full fees for them to attend there until they were 16 years old. My father thought it unlikely I would achieve any better success so he thought it a waste of time for me to bother seeking a scholarship, so I never took the scholarship exam.

I did, however, manage to pass the entrance examination to attend Taunton School, and, subsequently at 15 years, 11 months old, I had sufficient O'level passes to train for a minimum period of five years working as an articled clerk in a Chartered Accountants practice in Minehead. In the practice, there were three partners who oversaw the work produced by about thirty people in a general practice department. This was headed up by a senior manager and deputy manager, as well as employed qualified accountants and articled clerks who were training to be Chartered Accountants, supported by some secretaries. To become a fully qualified Chartered Accountant, it was necessary to pass three national examinations over five years. Sadly, many of my work colleagues did not make this, but I managed to scrape through. Virtually all the work for clients was spent in the chartered accountancy firm's office.

The work generally involved preparing accounts from the business income and expenditure recorded in cash books and supporting documentation supplied by each local client. These annual accounts would be submitted to the local H.M. Inspector of Taxes together with calculations of the taxes payable on the profits seeking Inland Revenue approval. If it was a limited company, the accounts would also need to be lodged at the UK's Companies House and also with the client's bank if they had bank loans or overdrafts to ensure there was sufficient cover to repay them in due course.

There was a wide difference between the separate types of businesses, virtually all of which were within a 20-mile radius, as the banks and nationally known high street businesses invariably employed national accountants and auditors rather than local ones. The clients dealt with locally included shopkeepers, farmers, tradesmen, garages, hotels and restaurants.

To my amazement, at 21 years of age, I was in line for a partnership in the local accountancy firm in Minehead. However, it was decided that, to obtain wider experience before returning later with the possibility of taking up the offer of partnership, I would first seek to join one of the then-Big-Eight-largest UK accountancy firms in London for three years. I then sought and was invited to interviews in London with two of the eight-largest accountancy firms in the UK and the World of Peat, Marwick, Mitchell & Co. ("Peat Marwick" is now KPMG) and Price Waterhouse, now "PWC" (which stands for PricewaterhouseCoopers).

To my further amazement, particularly as I had chosen to **not** go to university when I left school, I was offered employment as a newly qualified chartered accountant by both firms. I was very impressed with both firms but, as a country boy from Somerset,

I was more attracted to Peat Marwick. This was because Price Waterhouse, like several other large accountancy firms, had numerous specialised departments for dealing with company audits OR company taxation OR specialist assignments, like investigations for acquisitions OR dealing with insolvencies. The setup at Peat Marwick was very different with a mainly general practice, with departments acting like small firms, which dealt with all of the above, but with relatively small, specialist backup teams.

At the accountants' office in Somerset, there was a group of us who played in the local leagues of nine-pin-skittle bowling in special areas on the side of or above several pubs and clubs, each year. Our team name was called the Bowlers, and, at the start of the game, and, often longer, we would wear bowler hats.

This was very much a local activity played once a week for many weeks in the year, and I believe it is not usually played much outside West Somerset. The differences with the more-recently established ten-pin bowling are:

1. More space between the skittles so it was often possible for the ball to go straight through the middle without knocking over any other skittle.
2. Differing lengths between the bowling area and the skittles, depending on the space available.
3. Different types of ball with some being hard rubber and some wooden. No finger holes in the balls. Nine pins, rather than ten, are set up in a diamond shape at the end of the lane.
4. Each team's six players would throw his three balls twelve times in each game, and the cumulative scores were noted in chalk on a scoreboard. If the player knocked them all over in two balls, his score counted as nine plus the number he scored for his third ball. If he did it in one ball, for what was called a "flopper", he had two more scoring balls. Theoretically, he could score twenty-seven knocking over all nine pins three balls in a row, but that was extremely rare.

5. After each turn of three balls, the skittles would be manually reset by two individuals at the side of the pins who would stand them up again for the next player.
6. Every skittle room and alley was different in design in each pub.

After a couple of years, unbelievably, our youngish team won the second division, and, on promotion, amazingly, we won the first division two years later. This was much to the chagrin of the other local teams, many of whom viewed us as upstarts. Soon after, I left to work in London. Sadly, the team folded a few years later.

Early Years, Living in London

Having qualified as a chartered accountant in Somerset at 21 years of age, I was advised that it would be a good idea to spend three years in London gaining much wider experience. This would be useful before returning to Minehead to take up a partnership offered in the local accountancy firm.

Not surprisingly, life was very different in London in 1968. Knowing virtually nobody in London, I found cheap accommodation in a guest house in Highbury Grove, close to the Arsenal football ground. On many weekdays, I commuted daily by underground train from Highbury Grove tube station to Bank station and then walked to Peat, Marwick, Mitchell & Co's (now KPMG's) Ironmonger Lane office, just off Cheapside. However, for more than eighty per cent of the time, I went straight to the client's offices elsewhere to carry out audits, taxation and financial advisory work. The number of chairs in KPMG's office only accounted for less than a fifth of the total members of the department, as the remainder of the staff were meant to be working temporarily at client's offices where their books and records were kept.

On alternate weekends, I drove back and forth between London and Somerset to see my then-girlfriend, and, on the Saturday evening of the alternate weekend, I visited my cousin and her husband in Cheam in Surrey for a meal.

I knew very few people in London so I wanted to visit as many as possible of Football League team's home grounds in or near the city. I have many happy, lasting memories of many matches, save for the frightening experience of witnessing Millwall supporters throwing stones and other missiles at the visiting team's coach as they were leaving the ground after their match. Many windows were shattered but amazingly no significant injuries were reported.

Obviously, I saw as many of my favourite team Newcastle's matches with mixed success, but since my short time of residing in Highbury, I have also been keen on Arsenal. This was a novelty for me in London as I was used to having Football League teams being 40 miles away in Exeter and also two teams 60 miles away in Bristol, and it was too far to travel to their home matches.

On Wednesday evenings, in the Arsenal Tavern in Highbury Grove, there was often a talent night with a live band with the possibility of winning £1 on a clapometer basis. I sometimes participated with some saying I sang well but others told the truth!

Whilst I did sing to great applause the Tom Jones hit 'Green Grass of Home', my favourites were Jim Reeves' songs:

- 'I Love You Because'
- 'Welcome to My World'
- 'Adios Amigo'
- 'Am I Losing You'
- 'He'll Have to Go'

I was a little tearful the other day when Jim died and will always be grateful to him for earning me £2 singing his songs. It brought back many happy memories of a bygone era.

Of other songs, the easiest one to sing was 'Ob la Di, Ob la Da' originating with the Drifters but copied later by the Beatles. The secret is to choose a song to sing that is similar to the ones above, which do not have many highs and lows and hoping many in the audience will join in singing, particularly choruses, and this can cause much merriment. Amazingly, I did win a pound or two, but my thoughts of turning professional caused much disbelief amongst many others!

The highlight was being asked to appear as a guest singer at the Hammersmith Palais for a one-off guest performance on a Friday night in front of hundreds of partygoers. I greatly enjoyed the experience, particularly as it went down well with the big audience, and the backing group were great! Obviously, one chose fast moving songs for the audience to dance to, particularly those with the big choruses as the backing group would wade in to inflate the volume. The slower songs came towards the end of the performance when smooch time was more popular. Many advisors advised me to stick to my day job, although I have never been booed off cruise liners' talent competitions. Some say the audiences were too polite!

One advantage I gained is never being too frightened of speaking publicly (often live) with a microphone on several live radio and television appearances, commenting on the topic of critical matters in the media and entertainment world and their possible and/or likely outcomes, which I specialised in, and is covered in further chapters.

Early Years, Working for KPMG in London

Upon arriving in London from Somerset to work as a newly qualified chartered accountant at Peat, Marwick, Mitchell & Co. (now KPMG), I was allocated to one of the several general practice departments of about thirty to forty people. This had a senior manager, a deputy manager, some assistant managers and supervising seniors, some more junior qualified chartered accountants and articled clerks, mainly training straight after attending universities, and secretarial staff. The departments were named after each senior manager.

In many respects, unlike other accountancy firms, each of the numerous departments operated more like a small accountancy firm within itself, even though all of them were an individual part of a firm many times larger, overseen by the partners upstairs. The staff's work was mainly performed at clients' premises, and the departmental office area was quite small, so it was a big problem at certain periods, like holiday times, when clients did not choose to entertain their auditors or advisors. The general practice departments had access to the relatively few other specialist departments dealing with complicated tax and liquidations when required.

Eventually, I was promoted to a supervising senior accountant in 1971, heading up assignment teams of qualified accountants and articled clerks, and, in 1973, I became the deputy manager of a department involved in numerous client assignments, including National Westminster Bank. Four years later in 1977, I became the senior manager responsible for a whole department of thirty-five people named after me. Clients, amongst many others, included London Weekend Television (later merging into ITV) and the Rank Organisation, a very large media and entertainment group. In 1981, I was invited to join the KPMG

London partnership for the next nineteen years, a very distant dream of a country boy who did not go to university.

Some of the numerous assignments, up until I voluntarily left KPMG in 2000, are contained in several other chapters of this book. Many were outside London, in South East England, the United Kingdom and Europe. The highlight in London was being appointed to the UK, European and worldwide boards of KPMG, which employed over a million people, and, for a period, simultaneously as head of KPMG's Worldwide Marketing with huge multimillion-dollar and -pound budgets to spend on items over and above individual countries and continents. It was fun producing worldwide brochures on services provided.

Simultaneously, I was head of KPMG's Worldwide Information, Communications, Media and Entertainment practice employing many thousands of professional accountants and consultants dealing with those industries with substantial UK, European and worldwide budgets. Not surprisingly, the worldwide travel was huge and very time-consuming. However, most of it was fun and interesting, working with and meeting many talented men and women worldwide.

Working for Banks

National Westminster Bank

An audit client, in the Peat, Marwick, Mitchell & Co. (now KPMG) department I joined in 1968, was the newly established Big Four bank National Westminster Bank following the merge of the National Provincial Bank and the Westminster Bank. It had previously been one of the Big Eight banks in the UK prior to the merge.

Not many years afterwards, there was the not-unusual periodical downturn in the UK economy, and many bank customers had financial difficulty with property prices and the economy, generally, falling. A fair number owed numerous banks considerable sums of money, and the value of the security held by the bank was decreasing and becoming insufficient for a considerable number of customers to repay their debts.

I and my fellow manager reviewed a huge number of overdrafts and bank loans made to bank customers of National Westminster Bank to ensure proper provisions for losses were made. The dubious debts often included the words "property owners" to their normal business title of, for example, plumbers or shopkeepers and property owners.

This caused a major dilemma with calculating how much bank customers could afford to repay from their loans and overdrafts when the value of the security they had originally offered had decreased and did not cover the loan or overdraft advanced. This was substantial as there were more sellers than buyers for properties and other assets at that time. It was, therefore, far more difficult than usual for the bank to calculate how much they would eventually suffer in losses when the customers could not repay their loans or overdrafts. If those cumulative losses were significant enough, it could lead to the insolvency of numerous banks and other lenders. This leads to a mad rush from bank customers to extract monies before there becomes insufficient funds for them to do this. These downturns appear to have arisen periodically every twenty to thirty years in recent history and appears to be threatening to do this again at the time of writing this, in 2024.

N. M. Rothschild & Sons Limited (now Rothschild & Co)
I was always delighted to serve this multinational private and merchant bank controlled by the British and French branches of the Rothschild family, providing audit, tax and advisory services to this legendary bank, based in Bishopsgate near Liverpool Street train station in London. Relationships were very strong and, when some of their executives suggested to me an annual golf day for a Rothschild/KPMG match, this happened and was always cleared as appropriate by the London senior partner. This led to more than a decade of huge fun and banter about the respective merits of the two teams but the number of wins by both sides was always about equal.

Hambros Bank
One of the first clients I dealt with when I first came to London as a newly qualified accountant in 1968 was the audit and advisory work for Hambros Bank, based in Bishopsgate near Liverpool Street train station. Hambros was a British bank specialising in Anglo-Scandinavian business and had considerable expertise in trade finance and investment banking, and it was the sole banker to the Scandinavian kingdoms for many years. Several subsidiaries of the bank were dealing with different aspects of their business.

Henry Ansbacher Bank
Now known as Henry Ansbacher Holdings PLC, this was a merchant bank in the City of London that dealt mainly with processing transactions made by international trading companies. Lending money and bad debts were not really applicable. I was involved in the audit for several years.

Union Bank of the Middle East (UBME)
In 1982, I was assigned to work in Dubai for several months, virtually continuously seeking to stabilise the above bank and much of the United Arab Emirates economy. This is fully covered later in the "Overseas Assignment" chapter in this book.

Insolvencies
Other than the UBME above, this chapter does not include banks that appointed me to carry out receiverships and liquidations. These are included in the chapter on "Acting as a Receiver and Liquidator in the UK".

Working for Television Companies

Commencing in 1973, as a deputy manager at what is now KPMG, I started working, providing audit, accounting, tax and other advisory services, to several well-known British and American television companies. In 1981, I became the partner in charge of the audit and advisory work required by those companies for the next twenty years until I left KPMG.

London Weekend Television

My first experience in television was working as auditor and financial advisor for London Weekend Television (LWT), the London-based franchise holder for ITV Channel 3, broadcasting every Friday evening from 7 pm to 6 am on Monday mornings. This work was based mainly in their South Bank studios on the River Thames. At the time, Thames Television held the weekday London franchise other times each week for the same area, but I was not involved with them.

The income largely came from television advertising, the amounts for which varied to a large extent but were linked to the number in the audiences that resulted from the number of people viewing each programme as calculated by the independent Joint Industry Committee for Television Advertising Research (JICTAR). This meant it was very important to produce popular programmes. This was different from the BBC, whose mandate specified it needed to produce certain genres of programming for minority audiences as well as more popular programmes.

In its early stages, LWT sometimes did not achieve the very high ratings as often as desired, but audiences gradually recovered leading to increases in profits. This led to more popular entertainment programmes and more of its programmes broadcast on the ITV network nationally whilst not greatly increasing overall cost budgets.

In 1982, the first franchise period expired, and LWT had to reapply for its licence. At the time, I had been the KPMG external audit partner for a year having been the audit senior manager for several years before. This led to numerous very secretive meetings of a small number of people, in unusual and varying private locations, who were very conscious of ensuring the proposed tactics and detailed plans remained private and limited to only those people present. The rooms in which we were meeting were swept daily, in advance, for any devices that might have been planted by other potential television company competitors. It also meant that I could not discuss with any other KPMG partner or member of staff or any outsider what strategy was being planned and, even more, the amount of cash that was going to be in a sealed envelope attached to the bid. I knew that KPMG were assisting other ITV franchise bidders elsewhere in the UK as it was decreed that no other KPMG partner could take on any assignment in the UK without my clearance. Privately, we had to decline offers of acting for a number of different bidders as we had already signed with the incumbents or other bidders and would act for one only per franchise. In the event, we successfully retained LWT, Yorkshire and Granada, three of the Big Five. We also advised two other successful regional ITV companies and, then, perhaps not surprisingly, we became the auditors and advisors of ITV, as a whole, when, a few years later, the regional companies were consolidated into one overall national ITV franchise with regional operations as it is today.

It was also enjoyable for me to be the external auditor and advisor reviewing the costs incurred on some programmes outsourced by LWT to independent producers. These included *Midsomer Murders*, *Heartbeat* and *Doc Martin* and some others whilst I was still at KPMG.

As mentioned elsewhere, in the 1990s, there was an annual golf day with the LWT golf members and a KPMG golf team, led by me. This was fiercely contested and is mentioned in the "Golf" chapter of this book. After I left KPMG in 2000, I joined the LWT Golf Society as a member, and this continues up to the present day.

Also mentioned in the same chapter, I was given special permission from the senior partner at KPMG to play for the LWT second team when they were one player short on two occasions playing in the biennial three-day golf competition, called the *Natural Break*, between all the ITV regional companies.

Granada and Yorkshire Television

Under my leadership of KPMG's media and entertainment-industry practice, we enjoyed a very strong position in ITV in the UK with clients including three of the biggest five ITV companies as clients. In addition to London Weekend Television, these included Granada and Yorkshire Television.

Granada has always been well-known for producing the television soap programme *Coronation Street*, usually for six half-hour episodes each week generally on Mondays, Wednesdays and Fridays. The same is true for many decades for the Yorkshire soap programme *Emmerdale*, although they usually have at least one half-hour episode every weekday. Having witnessed the production of numerous television programmes around the world, I had always marvelled at how the two groups produce so many quality programmes for several hours each and every week. This is remarkable when a feature film lasting less than two hours often takes many months to produce. Granada and Yorkshire are now part of the unified ITV and were dealt with locally by the KPMG offices in Manchester and Leeds.

Chrysalis Television

When I left KPMG in 2000, I was invited to join the Board of Chrysalis Group, which had been a long-standing client of mine, as their external auditor. Whilst Chrysalis was well-known as a music company, its other subsidiaries included Chrysalis Television, dealing with several production companies comprising Red Rooster, Bentley, Cactus, Assembly, Lucky Dog, Chrysalis Sport, Watchmaker and Tandem as well as All 3 Media.

Some of their most popular programmes were the highly rated *Midsomer Murders*, *Heartbeat* and *Doc Martin*, several of which are still replayed on terrestrial television today having been so for some decades.

British Broadcasting Company

Finally, the irrefutable world-renowned BBC decided to put its audit out to external tendering in the 1990s. There was considerable discussion in KPMG whether this should be dealt with by our highly regarded media and entertainment practice as above or by KPMG's public sector practice, given the BBC had no outside shareholders. However, as we had such a strong presence in the ITV companies (leading to them all when they merged into one ITV, with KPMG retaining the work), I was quite prepared to differentiate it from the companies above. We were all delighted when this worked so, before Sky Television started, Channel 4 was the only terrestrial broadcaster that KPMG did not audit and provide financial services.

Independent Production Companies

Whilst most of our work for television companies was for large broadcasters worldwide, we also developed financial relationships with several independent companies in the UK and worked closely with the Independent Programme Producers Association (IPPA), Association for Independent Producers (AIP) and Producers Association for Cinema and Television (PACT). Several of their larger members became clients of KPMG. Not long afterwards, the chief executive of PACT came to work for me at KPMG, providing financial consultancy services and was joined by the editor of the weekly *Broadcast* magazine. This meant we could provide expanded financial services to a very wide group of film and television companies in the UK.

NBC Television

For several decades, the KPMG firm in the United States acted as auditors and advisors to the National Broadcasting Company

(NBC), one of the three largest television companies in the United States. For numerous decades, it had been owned by General Electric, one of the largest companies in America.

In the 1990s, its legendary chairman, Jack Welch, became concerned that the NBC management was too greatly focused on broadcasting in the United States and not concerned enough about broadcasting worldwide. This was despite the fact that, even though NBC has regularly been a sponsor of the Olympic Games and televised the games in the United States, the company produced them for elsewhere in the world.

Welch wished to form a relatively small international committee to advise how best his business could be expanded outside the Americas. NBC's auditors in the United States – my KPMG partner – recommended to Jack that, as I was the chairman of KPMG's Worldwide Media and Entertainment Group, and consequently attended many worldwide television events, I would, therefore, be a good candidate to join the committee. On being approached, I was more than happy to do so as, to me, it was a privilege. This was on the basis that I was acting as an international specialist and had no part in personally acting for NBC on any other assignments carried out by KPMG. A further condition placed on the committee was that, at the outset, it should meet at least twice yearly in different places around the world but not at all in the United States. This was because Jack thought that some of his executives considered the United States to *be* the whole world and that anything that happened outside of it was barely relevant. The committee changed all of this, and it appears that NBC has since gone from strength to strength.

The quality of the people on the committee (except for me!) was of the highest quality and, as well as advising and discussing with them, they were very enjoyable people to meet and work with, even if their international travel was not huge. Whilst I had a lot to give, I learnt plenty as well as what was going on in the world of broadcasting. This committee met periodically for several years leading to clear conclusions on the way ahead but, after a few years, it became increasingly difficult to consistently come up with new original ideas as they had probably been previously considered. It was a great honour to help a great company and chairman, who had many similar characteristics to my father's. I never charged for my time, but I certainly earned some huge respect from the worldwide NBC management who often called me for an open discussion some years after.

Working for Film Companies

The Rank Organisation's Film Group
The Rank Organisation was a large Stock Exchange-listed company with several different divisions, one of which was its Film and Television Division. This included Rank Film Distributors, Rank Film Laboratories, Pinewood Studios and Rank Advertising Films. Odeon Cinemas was part of the Rank Organisation Group, but I did not specifically deal with this cinema company directly as Rank deemed it to be in its Leisure division rather than in its Film and Television Group division.

I became the external auditor and external advisor of Rank's Film Division for several years, from 1981, and attended its various locations for consecutive days in an early week in November each year to review the work carried out by the KPMG group of auditors involved at each location. It was great to have special staff escorts to visit any area of their activity, when members of the public would not normally be allowed to most areas of the operations.

It was necessary to start at 8 am each day with the intention of finishing the review before having a meeting with the relevant company's chief executive and finance director at around 12 noon. For several years, at Pinewood Studios, I would meet with the legendary Cyril Howard, head of the studios. Coincidentally, Cyril was brought up in the West Country by some of my parents' best friends.

Most of the time, there was relatively little to discuss as their work was usually exemplary, although there were often a few points that needed discussion and clarification before being resolved. Upon conclusion of the meetings, there was always a sumptuous lunch at a nearby location at the completion of the annual visit.

Other Film Companies
In addition to the above, in the 1980s and 1990s, I headed up my specialist team acting as a financial advisor of several

independent film production and distribution companies. These included Working Title Films (including *Four Weddings and a Funeral*, *The Tall Guy*, *My Beautiful Laundrette*, *Notting Hill* and *The Borrowers*), London Film Productions (including *Lady Chatterly* and *I, Claudius*) and Chrysalis Visual Entertainment (including eight other production companies). Obtaining finance was often far from easy due to the risky nature of making most films and the consequent lack of security to financiers if the film was not a great success. However, we remained supportive of the Independent Programme Producers Association and the Producers Alliance for Cinema and Television, and there were a number of notable highlights.

The talent in the United Kingdom is outstanding given the small size of the country, geographically, and, together with numerous other industry clients, I was delighted to be involved in such a significant way.

The Cannes Film Festival
Obviously, as head of KPMG's Worldwide Media and Entertainment Practice, it was a necessity for me to attend the annual Cannes Film Festival in May for several years. Contrary to the three other worldwide media and entertainment annual events held in Cannes – being two worldwide television events and one worldwide music event occurring in January, April and October – this event was produced by many film companies in large hotel suites and not with stands in the Palais. Obviously, it was more difficult to arrange meetings, and there was considerable interest in talent spotting by members of the public

National Film and Television School
For several years in the 1990s, I was pleased to be invited to act as a periodic financial tutor to students at the National Film and Television School. My role was to give them advice about the financial aspects of the film industry, where the funds might be available to finance productions and the necessary steps that were needed to access those funds. This advice was designed to

help them develop their own business plans, and other aspects, that were necessary for putting together all the matters needed for a successful application for finance.

Several students had originally assumed that if they had some ideas for a new film production, finance would be easy. However, the students needed to appreciate that if the film was not a great success, the financiers had little security to fall back on. It was generally necessary for their production ideas to be treated as a normal business plan, and it would be helpful to have some private backers, meaning that less than 100 per cent of the funds needed to be externally financed.

Acting as Receiver and Liquidator in the UK

Peat, Marwick, Mitchell and Co. ('Peat Marwick' is now KPMG) have dealt with numerous receiverships, administrations and liquidations in the UK for numerous decades with several of them famous, like Rolls-Royce. As insolvencies occurred on an irregular basis, sometimes due to the state of the nation's economy, the firm's structure had a relatively small specialist insolvency department, which primarily dealt with liquidations, some of the smaller receiverships and, in more recent years, administrations.

When there were substantial receiverships and administrations involving numerous staff, they would call on the general practice departments of the firm to provide substantial numbers of staff to lead or assist in the insolvency team for that assignment. In 1975, there was a periodical downturn in various industries in the UK, particularly in the property industry. In a short period of time, one of the very largest UK housebuilders, Northern Developments, and another large housebuilder, Bacal Construction, one of the largest particularly in the South Midlands, both fell into receivership and Peat, Marwick, Mitchell and Co. (now KPMG) were appointed as receivers and managers to both. For the summer of 1975, the accounting firm was collectively one of the largest housebuilders in England as a whole.

Bacal Construction
Bacal Construction personally appointed me to lead the team seeking to raise as much money as possible to repay the banks' owed money. The banks had lent substantial sums to finance the purchase of the land and the construction costs for the housebuilding activities. For some six months, I led the team raising as much money net as possible from the demise. We inherited a substantial amount of properties in various stages of development. My father and my two brothers were engaged

in housebuilding in Somerset and their informal advice to me was extremely helpful.

Following advice, I took the view that, if, on any property, planning permission had been granted, construction had commenced and was above the damp proof course level a short height above the surface, we would seek to retain sufficient staff to complete the construction of each property as this would produce the higher net proceeds above solely selling the land value. If construction had not reached the damp proof course level, we would sell the property as land only. We had to offer a bonus to all the employees necessary to retain them as everybody knew they would have to look for other jobs when all the unfinished houses were completed and sold as we would not be buying any new plots of land for development.

My team and I were based in Northampton at least four days each week for several months until the construction was completed. We were very open with the staff to be released on overall timetables so they had as much notice as possible.

Many millions were recovered for the banks and amounted to about eight per cent more than the minimum number expected at the outset. However, it was sad to work for quite a while with a large number of talented tradesmen who lost their jobs through no fault of their own.

Minns and Cranes Music

I was appointed by Barclays Bank as the receiver and manager of Minns and Cranes Music, a family-run business that owned numerous musical instrument shops in England. Some shops were well known, for example, the Liverpool shop and the in-store musical shop in Harrods. With a head office in Bournemouth, the business had been run very successfully for many years by a father who, when approaching retirement, passed the business over to his son. His son lacked his father's business acumen, and substantial losses arose.

It was clear that several of the leasehold businesses were likely to continue making losses, and it would be virtually impossible to trade on at a profit as a whole. These stores were closed after a short period of selling the stock. Some of the stores were trading at a profit, particularly the in-store music store in Harrods, and trading even continued whilst being advertised for sale. It attracted considerable interest, including from Richard Branson, as described in the chapter in this book about working with him. The purchaser was the Chrysalis Group, one of the leading UK music, radio and television companies.

There are two postscripts to this receivership:

1. Coincidentally, I joined the Board of the Stock Exchange-listed company, Chrysalis, as a non-executive director several years later, when I left KPMG in 2000.
2. To save time and money, a member of KPMG's staff, who was assisting the wind-down and sell-off, travelled daily from KPMG's Southampton Office. At the small function at the end of the assignment, she met Douglas (now, Sir Douglas) Flint, who was dealing solely with the sell-off of the profit making shops. They got married a short time later. Douglas later became chairman of HSBC Holdings until 2017.

Unusual and Unique Overseas Assignments

When one works for a major international firm of accountants and financial consultants, it is likely and often inevitable, for one reason or another, that there will be UK, European and Worldwide travel to carry out work when the assignment is unusual or the client does not wish the work to be carried out by the local firm for one reason or another. The same is amplified when a UK practitioner becomes a board member of the committee responsible for a continent's or worldwide activities that will meet quarterly for a few days. The venues are rarely the same as in the recent past.

It is also true that, when a particular project is unusual in nature and/or exceptionally large, local offices will need assistance to carry out the work. In these circumstances the concept of sitting at the same desk every working day for a fixed time in a week does not apply here as it is totally different from that applicable to smallish firms of accountants or businesses dealing solely within their local area.

This chapter deals with some unique and unusual non-committee assignments in the following countries where not a large number of UK citizens would visit for work or vacation:

- Sudan
- Kuwait
- Japan
- Dubai
- Saudi Arabia
- Hong Kong

I also dealt, for a short time, with an insolvency in Paris, which was solely to close down the business of two young UK citizens who had bought properties on the Avenue des Champs-Élysées.

Property prices had fallen, and it was necessary to sell the properties to repay non-extendable mortgage amounts. The properties had also devalued in local currency, which had not been fixed in advance.

Khartoum in Sudan

In November 1973, at their Sixth Arab Summit Conference, the eighteen Arab countries that were members of the League of Arab States resolved to set up The Arab Bank for Economic Development of Africa, otherwise known as BADEA. This was an acknowledgement that they were financially much better off due to their oil revenues while most of the African countries did not enjoy such revenues and were relatively poor. Those eighteen Arab countries also resolved to set up the Head Office in Khartoum, the capital of the Republic of Sudan in the middle of Africa, roughly halfway between the Arab countries and the very South of Africa.

The Establishing Agreement was signed in February 1974, and it was resolved that the Arab Bank would be an independent international institution that could enjoy full international legal status and complete autonomy in administrative and financial matters. It had a mandate to stimulate the contribution of Arab capital to African countries, to participate in financing economic development in Africa and to participate in providing technical assistance required for the development of Africa.

The question arose as to how African countries would access these substantial profits that the Arab Countries made. The local KPMG office in Khartoum was delighted to be appointed to set up the full details of how African businesses could access these very generous and available funds. However, they did not believe that they had the international qualifications to carry out all the skills required. They sought external assistance from KPMG's London office personnel to draft the manual that discussed how to access the funds. I was appointed to lead the team of three, with Chris Collingwood and Richard Horsley from

London office providing the assistance. This was an eight-week assignment in Khartoum.

The work was very interesting and quite challenging; although, it was a similar process to provide start-up finance for businesses needed anywhere in the world. Obviously, there was the necessary requirement for potential recipients to prepare credible, detailed business plans with clear objectives, costs, timetables and full details of the project and how it would work. The benefits needed to be the introduction of goods and services that were not already available. The local need for such a project was also key. Also, ensuring the potential for the type of business that required the funding could be achieved with the availability of suitable, qualified personnel to implement the plan. Plus, a key issue was assessing the local demands for the availability, qualifications and output of the appropriate personnel due to be employed. Sensible financial projections of when break-even would be achieved had to be assessed, as well as to how potential surpluses would be produced to create viable long-term businesses.

I was permitted to come home to the UK after four weeks (halfway through the assignment) for a one-week break to spend time with my wife and very young family. The local senior partner of KPMG's Khartoum office had previously asked me if, upon my return, I would agree to be the best man at the wedding of the son of one of the office's biggest clients. This apparently was the local custom at weddings in the Sudan where the best man has to be previously unknown to anybody who attends the wedding. He was very keen to ensure that I was definitely going to return to Sudan as finding a replacement at such short notice would have been difficult.

I did return on time but shortly afterwards, I and my two London colleagues went to work one day and, as usual, we went to the (British) Sudan Club for lunch. There were soon very loud noises not far away, and it very soon became clear that Khartoum was being invaded, it turned out to be by the Libyans. Khartoum is like London and has many bridges crossing its major river. The

River Nile divides Khartoum from Omdurman. The noise of gunfire was extremely loud and appeared very close. We soon realised that it was going to be too dangerous to try to get back to our hotel in the local high street. I slept that night in various positions in the men's sporting changing room. It was impossible to sleep with the noise, but cat-napping occasionally was possible. The following morning, there were several bullet holes in the changing room I had tried to sleep in on the benches. I felt like a cat who had just used one of my nine lives. I was reunited with my colleagues who were unharmed after sleeping in other rooms in the club. Unbelievably, the gunfire subsided relatively quickly and, incredibly, the Libyans, after having apparently captured and controlled all Khartoum and Omdurman roads, had decided to go home.

I did act as the best man at the wedding, which was a unique experience. In accordance with local custom, I had to have the first dance with the bride doing the local penguin-style dance. I am glad it was not recorded!

We duly finished the assignment in the eight weeks, which has led to the unbelievable success of BADEA. When the bank began operations in March 1975, it started with $250 million US in its first three years, and its revenues for three years have now increased to reach $350 million US in 2019 for financing development projects, technical assistance and exports. BADEA has been a great success over its forty-nine years, providing much-needed monies, by my rough calculation, totalling approximately $13 billion US.

Whilst writing this chapter, I was saddened to hear about civil war breaking out again in Khartoum, and so many residents and visitors have had to flee the city by any means available. Foreign countries have made special flights and other arrangements to assist their citizens escape Khartoum.

Kuwait and Japan

If and when people are discussing unusual countries they have visited, one of my favourite questions for amusement is, 'How many taxpayers do you think there are in the State of Kuwait?'

This would cover income tax, companies' corporation tax, capital gains tax, value-added tax and all other taxes. Amazement usually follows when I say that the answer is very, very few and far lower than virtually all other companies in the world. Increased interest is expressed about, for starters, there being no personal income tax imposed on Kuwaiti nationals and, I believe, many other Arab nationals. Neither has there been any indirect taxes until, I believe, very recently when a five per cent value-added tax commenced on 1 April 2021.

For company corporation tax, no tax is payable by companies wholly owned by Kuwaiti nationals or those owned by Bahrain, Oman, Qatar, Saudi Arabia and the United Arab Emirates. There is, however, a rate of fifteen per cent for foreign-owned businesses – a rate somewhat below many other countries in the world. The principal reason for these relatively low rates of taxation is that the Kuwaiti Government raises huge revenues having nationalised the two most northerly oilfields in the Persian Gulf. The State, therefore, receives the huge net revenues from all the profits of these two operations, so there is no point in taxing them when they are so clearly within Kuwaiti territory.

However, there is a third oilfield situated offshore in the very south of Kuwait, just north of the very narrow Straits of Hormuz. The concession for this oilfield is operated by the Japanese-owned and Tokyo Stock Exchange-listed company Arabian Oil Company (AOC). The oilfield is situated offshore at Ras al Khafji in a seven-mile neutral zone. This area exists because the zone borders Kuwait to the north and Saudi Arabia to the south. Both countries claim they own this neutral zone, but the dispute has never been resolved so neither country can justify nationalisation.

Consequently, it is unavoidable that AOC has to pay huge taxes to both Saudi Arabia and Kuwait governments as neither country can nationalise the oilfield. The total taxes paid annually to the two countries is believed to be at least ninety per cent of net income from the oil extraction from the Gulf, but the remainder still contributed a substantial amount to the Japanese Stock Exchange-listed company.

It is believed that this oilfield is of major significance to Japan as I have been informed that Japan has little to no oil in its own territorial waters, and, without this important supply from Kuwait/Saudi Arabia, it would have to go on to the international market to obtain its necessary supply. This would lead to the cost potentially going sky high. Furthermore, it would not take a lot to block the quite narrow Straits of Hormuz not far south of the AOC oilfield, and Japan would then have to go on to the international market to satisfy its oil needs and that would likely to be very expensive. It is often believed that this is why Japan often remains relatively silent on international disputes at, for example, United Nations meetings.

For several years, I visited the dreadfully filthy neutral zone in the desert each February. I would fly to Kuwait City and then travel some eighty miles down the Gulf to review the work carried out by my two KPMG colleagues, who had worked there for a few previous weeks. On our return to Kuwait City, before flying home, we would meet with the local Kuwaiti Government officials to discuss our findings for the visit and matters outstanding from the year since our previous visit. Other than the government officials and the hotel receptionists in Kuwait City, very few local residents of Kuwait spoke any English, so verbal communication, locally, was very difficult.

The second half of the annual assignment was to visit Tokyo in June each year to match the enhanced monetary amount for the figures of oil extracted with those obtained in Kuwait and to finalise our opinion on the company's tax return, submitted to the Kuwaiti Government. Very few local residents, except hotel receptionists, speak English, so verbal communication was some of the most difficult I have experienced in the world. Moreover, Japan's written word is totally different with characters.

It was mandatory to have a daily update meeting to deal with our observations and questions before finishing work each weekday at 5 pm when the office effectively closed. As might be expected, the local officials would seek tax deductibility for various new items, virtually all of which would be denied as they had little or insufficient merit, and the Japanese would often recoil in disappointment. We would then return to the nearby five-star Imperial Hotel for a shower, etc. and then be collected at 6 pm by two of the senior Arabian Oil Company local personnel. We would then be taken to one of the large number of small bars in Tokyo. These bars could only accommodate not much more than a dozen people with a lady behind the bar. The whole bar was less than fifteen feet wide and 45 feet long in total, with some customers sitting on bar stools.

There are so many bars of this size in Tokyo as so many local workers, who had finished their work for the day, choose not to go home at the earliest time as their wives would be of the opinion that their husbands were not working hard enough to gain promotions, and that they were not earning enough to enhance the family's financial position.

At 7 pm, we would then go for a nice dinner with mainly Japanese-type food, like sushi, which, thankfully, I generally enjoyed, even though it was quite different from normal English food. At 8 pm, it was mandatory to go to one of the large number of karaoke establishments where a hostess would sit with us, ensuring our glasses were topped up (even when little had been drunk from them) and propositioning the attendees to entertain everyone with singing karaoke. If one was a fast drinker, getting drunk would have been very quick, so sipping, rather than swigging, was a good idea.

It was not an option not to sing every evening and preferably twice. However, having previously made several guest-singing appearances at Arsenal Tavern in Highbury Grove when I had first come to London and, having won more than one weekly talent competitions with the residents' band there and also having done a guest experience at O2 Shepherd's Bush Empire in West London, this was not as daunting to me as it probably was for many visitors to Tokyo. My favourite song was the relatively monosyllabic *Ob La Di, Ob La Da*, which always went down well in addition to some of the great Jim Reeves songs (which put everybody to sleep!). It invariably went down well, particularly as listeners would usually join in for the chorus.

Whilst the entertainment was unique and enjoyable, it was necessary to remain professional about the hospitality without it affecting our judgement on our work for the Kuwaiti Government.

From my time in Japan, I have binding memories that many office officials and other workers didn't go straight home after finishing work at, say, 5.30 pm, as they do in the Western World. If they did, their wives would believe they are not working hard enough to earn any kind of promotion that would enhance the family's future finances. Since their offices are locked up soon after 5.30 pm, heading to any of the nearby and numerous bars was a way of life for them. Two hours or so later, they would catch their trains home. Sometimes I wish I worked permanently in Japan!

In the final year of my visits, I was approached by AOC's chief executive, who invited me to play a round of golf one day. Obviously, I had not brought my clubs, etc. with me coming from the UK, but it was easy to hire some locally. We played a very cordial and pleasant round of golf, which very, very few foreigners would ever have the opportunity to enjoy, due to the rarity of golf courses. I believe Japan is seventy per cent mountainous, so large homes are virtually non-existent. Many golfers have to settle exclusively for indoor driving ranges. After the round of golf, as an extra great privilege, I was invited to a late lunch back at the chief executive's home. Despite being one of the highest-paid executives in Japan, I was amazed his home was a two-bedroom-sized house as seen in housing estates in the UK, with his outside space limited to a seven-foot-wide concrete patio.

Dubai

The largest and most significant corporate recovery/insolvency assignment I ever worked on was in the early part of 1982 when there was a very serious financial crisis in Dubai, one of the United Arab Emirates.

Two of the Galadari brothers had fallen out with the third brother, Abdul Wahab Galadari, and both sides went on a huge splurge of purchasing or establishing a double-figure number of significant different types of businesses on a copycat basis. Abdul Wahab acquired one of the local banks (the Union Bank of the Middle East (UBME)), and the other two brothers also acquired another significant local bank. As a further example, Abdul Wahab acquired the Hyatt hotel franchise, and his brothers acquired the Hilton hotel franchise. One side owned the *Gulf News*, and the other owned another local daily newspaper. This mirror image stretched to close to twenty different types of local businesses, including several local franchises of major international companies.

Unfortunately, the money spent on the copycat acquisitions of these mainly leading businesses was funded mainly by depositors' monies lodged with the two local banks rather than shareholders monies. This is outlawed by the governing bodies of most countries in the world where banks are generally forbidden to use depositors' monies to make loans to directors and are required to establish and maintain sufficient cash reserves to ensure depositors can always access their funds without financial strain.

It did not take long to limit depositors on how much money they could withdraw from their accounts, and, on some days, virtually none could be withdrawn as the bank did not have the necessary resources available, and a moratorium of limits was in use.

There is always an issue when banks get into financial trouble worldwide as an adverse external auditors' report is likely to lead to a rush of depositors to extract their monies out of a financial institution. This inevitably leads to the financial collapse of the institution, which then has a significant domino effect on the financial fortunes of the local community when nobody has any liquidity in its cash resources.

The young and very able Dubai Government's Minister of Finance, Mohamed al Tahir, who had gone to university in

England, called in KPMG, and I was asked to be part of leading the team of nearly twenty accountants, residing in Dubai, called in by the local KPMG office mainly from London. This was necessary as the local office had only limited resources for such a large assignment: to bail out the economy and solve the crisis in the Emirate. Accommodation was easy as one part of the major hotels that we were managing had achieved a sale; it was the excellent Hyatt Hotel with an ice rink on the ground floor by reception, and I had a nice bedroom overlooking the foyer.

It was clear that several businesses were unviable and posting losses often, particularly the smaller ones, so they were closed down relatively quickly as to have them carry on would have only worsened the situation, and buyers at a significant price were unlikely.

However, several of the businesses were viable, including the local *Gulf News* daily newspaper, which still publishes today. The Jumerah Hyatt hotel is still operating impressively today even though Dubai has grown extensively on the other side of the centre with the very impressive Palms area built on reclaimed land. The viable businesses were sold as going concerns and substantially reduced the debt level that needed to be covered.

Bit by bit, and with close cooperation with the Government of Dubai, the good businesses survived, the depositors' monies were covered, and the economy survived for several years until the following recession. Dubai has a boom and bust financial history where there is rapid growth followed by a collapse. Some years later, the economy recovers and the partly built buildings from the previous collapse are finalised. This has been followed some years later by the next overdevelopment, which triggers more partly built buildings.

It has always been a fantastic experience to visit the lovely Dubai, and it will always have a very special place in my heart for the great Emirate it has become. This is very laudable.

Staffing KPMG's Middle East Firm

Under the worldwide constitution of KPMG, the London office was responsible for the management and the recruitment of qualified accountants to staff the firm's various local Middle East offices. This was because there was insufficient qualified local candidates to carry out the work for clients in the Dubai, Abu Dhabi, Bahrain, Qatar and Sharjah offices. As I had been on previous assignments in most of those Gulf States, I assisted on the recruitment in London to fill the gap.

Saudi Arabia

One of the shortest assignments I ever experienced in the world was when the Jeddah KPMG office in Saudi Arabia called into the London office to find a way to resolve a liquidity deficiency issue in the local Nissan/Datsun dealer's business. These cars were very popular throughout the Middle East at the time, and the number of sales was at a record high.

Sharia law is very different from that of most of the Western World, and there was no legislation for liquidations, receiverships and other insolvencies. I had no idea how long it would take to resolve the issue, but I agreed to visit Jeddah to see if I could help.

It took less than one day to realise the problem was that the Saudi Arabian Riyal had devalued against the Japanese Yen, and, without updating exchange rates in fixing sale prices, every car sold was at a loss in the local currency. This was immediately adjusted for future sales and the business subsequently prospered. My family and the KPMG London and Jeddah offices were delighted to have me home so soon.

Hong Kong

In the early 1990s, I received a telephone call from KPMG's Hong Kong office saying that the then-Governor of Hong Kong, the Right Honourable Christopher Patten, had reported to them that he was receiving a huge number of complaints from local residents about the poor quality and the very limited choice of television channels available in the territory. At the time, there were just two local channels broadcasting in Cantonese and two broadcasting in English. Upon investigation, it was obvious that the local and many television productions on all four channels were in exceptionally poor quality and choice – way behind what was available in most civilised countries in the world.

The Hong Kong KPMG office did not have the specialist industry knowledge to alleviate the position so, as the chairman of KPMG's UK, European and Worldwide Media and Entertainment Practice, I was invited to fly out with two colleagues from our specialist UK-media-consulting practice to see what could be done. Soon after arriving, we met the local government officials who were seeking a solution. After writing down their detailed instructions, I returned to London and left my two colleagues to progress the consultancy assignment.

The key factor was that Hong Kong is a very heavily populated area of only 1,100 square miles, only two-thirds the size of London. It did not take long to realise that our recommendation and best solution was to dig up every road in Hong Kong in as short a timescale as possible and lay the cable that could subsequently potentially carry the whole range of local and international television channels to all residents. Many channels would be free to air and others available through subscriptions. Satellite television was thought to not be the best solution as it was in many other countries in the world.

As a result of our recommendation, Wharf Cable Television was incorporated in June 1993 and granted the licence to offer a broad range of information and entertainment channels throughout Hong Kong. It offered over 100 pay-television channels, with fifty-four being operated by what became the publicly listed Hong Kong Cable Television in October 1998.

I always remember that, on my second visit to Hong Kong, midway through the assignment, I received a request from the British governor to visit him at his premises at The Peak of Hong Kong. Naturally, there was the feeling that he might have some concerns on how the project was progressing. I sat down in his lovely lounge overlooking most of the whole territory and enjoyed a cup of coffee. He expressed his grateful thanks for the swift progress that was being made, and he had been advised that the work was ahead of schedule. He had only one concern. His daughters had asked him what programmes they could hopefully watch, in the future, which were not available for them to watch, in the past, and he wanted to give them a realistic answer. I promised him a response before the end of the day and, when doing this, I handed him the full list of about 100 channels that would shortly be available for viewing. He was delighted that his daughters and Hong Kong residents were going to be happier in the future.

Hong Kong Cable Television has since prospered, originally targeting middle class subscribers but later, with lowered prices, attracting working class subscribers and cheaper phone services and internet access. It now has more than a half-million current subscribers.

Working for Newspapers

The Observer Newspaper
In 1981, Lonrho purchased the UK's Sunday national newspaper, *The Observer*. As KPMG were the auditors and financial advisors to the Lonrho Group, KPMG were appointed the same at *The Observer*. At the time, I was a newly appointed partner in KPMG's London office and already had numerous media and entertainment clients, several of which are mentioned elsewhere in this book. I was duly appointed as the partner in charge of the audit, tax and financial advisory work for *The Observer*.

The Observer was the world's first Sunday newspaper when it was first published in 1791 and had the most widely read newspaper website and app for news. It was named as the National Newspaper of the Year at the British Press Awards in 2007.

On top of doing the requisite work to audit *The Observer*'s accounts, it was necessary to confirm the amount of individual newspapers that had been sold each month. This was effectively making available to advertisers the number of newspapers sold monthly as this was the basis for the advertising income in each production. It was necessary to deduct the number of individual papers unsold from the number of individual newspapers printed and distributed. This was not always easy.

The Observer became part of the Guardian Media Group in 1993 when my work for *The Observer* ceased.

The *Today* Newspaper
In March of 1986, Eddy (a.k.a. Selim Jehan) Shah launched the freesheet *Today* newspaper as a free daily newspaper, and he planned for it to be a rival to the long-established *Daily Mail* and *Daily Express* newspapers. The latter two newspapers were not free. Due to its production methods, it forced the conversion of all the national newspapers to electronic production and colour

printing. KPMG client Lonrho bought the *Today* newspaper four months after first publication, and I became the external partner in charge of the audit and advisory services.

The *Sunday Today* newspaper was launched in 1986 but closed within a year as it could not attract sufficient advertisers to achieve a trading profit. The *Today* newspaper ceased publication in November 1995 after considerable losses.

Working for UK Radio Companies

The radio industry in the UK and elsewhere in the world is often perceived by many to be the poor relation to television for news and entertainment programmes. However, the number of listeners is remarkably high as there are numerous jobs and locations in the world where it is not possible to watch television programmes, but it is possible to listen to radio programmes during the daytime, as well as the evenings. This includes, for example, when driving cars and at workplaces where a television could be a distraction to the work being carried out, but sometimes a radio channel could well be permitted and appreciated.

When I became the KPMG audit partner in charge of the audit and financial advisory work for one of the leading music companies worldwide, Chrysalis, Heart Radio was in the group in addition to the Chrysalis music company based in London. There were numerous other significant regional commercial radio stations spread across the United Kingdom, which were KPMG audit or financial-advisory clients, and these were locally advised by my fellow partners and myself.

As well as being well-known as a world-class television broadcaster, the BBC is recognised also as one of the best broadcaster worldwide of radio programmes. In the 1990s, KPMG were listed as one of the accounting firms invited to tender for the whole of the BBC audit and financial-advisory work. Adding the several local commercial radio stations, including Classic FM, Virgin, Capital, Heart and Gold, as well as many other regional companies, KPMG clients were broadcasting daily to about seventy per cent of the whole of the UK's population by radio as well as television.

In view of this situation on behalf of KPMG, we sponsored various events at the Radio Festival, held every couple of years and attended by key executives from the industry.

Subsequently, the chief executive of the Radio Academy, representing all of the UK's radio industry, John Bradford, accepted my employment offer, and he joined KPMG to give financial and other industry advice across the board to key radio executives.

In 2000, I left KPMG and, amongst several other appointments, I was appointed as a non-executive main board director of Chrysalis Group plc, and therefore, I became directly involved in several media and entertainment businesses, including Heart Radio.

Soon after, I was knighted as a Fellow of the UK's Radio Academy and remain so at the time of writing.

Working with Chris Wright CBE, Sir George Martin and The Chrysalis Group

In 1985, I was appointed as partner in charge of the external audit and advisor of Chrysalis Group, a Stock Exchange-listed music and television production group, and thus remained as such until 2000, when I left KPMG. I immediately joined Chrysalis's board of directors as a non-executive director and continued until 2010.

The chairman was Chris Wright, who was very experienced in finding and promoting music recording artists. The group's non-executive directors included the now-Sir George Martin, the legendary recording manager. As with Chris, George was outstanding in identifying new talent in the music industry, and they were famous for overseeing the recordings of numerous artists and promotion of pop groups to ensure, as far as possible, that they produced hit records. George was the recording manager for The Beatles and many other pop groups. Chris had vast experience in the music industry. I had a fair amount of previous experience with other music companies, like Virgin Records, and preparing industry valuations.

Other Chrysalis acts included Spandau Ballet, Jethro Tull, Blondie, Leo Sayer, Billy Idol, Procul Harum and Ultravox. It was a pleasure working with Chris and Sir George and the other directors. The group set up and supported several independent television programme companies. These are listed in the "Working for Television" chapter of this book. Chrysalis also formed Chrysalis Radio, including Heart Radio broadcasting in the London area.

The role of a non-executive director and Finance Committee member is to ensure that reliable up-to-date figures are available, the company is on track to match its annual forecast agreed in advance and that shareholders are kept frequently properly informed. The management at Chrysalis were generally excellent at doing this.

In November 2010, after an original rejected bid, the German Bertelsman Music Group and Kohlberg Kravis and Roberts (KKR) made an offer (Chrysalis' second offer) of £160 per share for all the shares in Chrysalis, valuing the company at £107.4 million. This was accepted.

It was great to work directly with two legends in the global music industry for some twenty-five years before stepping down.

Working with Sir Richard Branson and The Virgin Group of Companies

As mentioned in the chapter on UK insolvencies, in the 1980s, I was appointed as receiver and manager of Minns and Cranes Music Limited by the bank that had lent money, on a secured-loan basis, to that company. Minns and Cranes sold numerous kinds of musical instruments in over twenty shops all over England and had the Harrods in-store concession in Knightsbridge in London.

As receivers and managers, it is normal to continue to trade on shops and other businesses that are potentially cash-flow positive as payments due to past creditors are suspended for the time being. To do this means that the business must realise net-cash funds from selling assets, like the stock held in the stores, to raise money to increase later payments to past creditors. The hope is that it sells all or several of its shops as 'going concern' businesses, and this will normally raise far more cash than shutting down the business and selling the assets piecemeal.

This was done for a while, but several leased Minns and Cranes shops were closed as they were not cash-flow positive. However, the Harrods store facility was one of several we chose to continue trading and was advertised as a going concern and subsequently sold.

Not unsurprisingly, we accepted the highest offer, which was from the Chrysalis Group, whose shares were listed on the London Stock Exchange. Richard (now Sir Richard) Branson, chairman of the Virgin Group of Companies, rung me up, asking me why his bid was not accepted. When we subsequently met on his office boat in North West London, I said to him that he was not the highest bidder, and, as receiver and manager, I had no choice but to accept the Chrysalis offer and could not sell the business to him.

Richard then mentioned that he thought his privately owned Virgin Group of Companies had gotten to the size where he needed a bigger accounting firm to help him expand his empire. I happily accepted his request, and, then for fifteen years, up to 2000, oversaw the KPMG team, featuring Robert Allison, to assist him in continuing to build a substantial empire of companies internationally under the Virgin Group of Companies label.

It was clear that to strengthen his expanding internal team, he needed to upgrade his accounting staff, and when asked, I agreed that Trevor Abbott should be considered for appointment as Group Finance Director. He subsequently became Group Managing Director with Richard as the executive chairman. Trevor had previously worked with me at KPMG before moving to Management Agency and Music, the company famous for managing Tom Jones and Engelbert Humperdinck and several other artists.

The Virgin Group grew rapidly, enhancing numerous worldwide businesses, including Virgin Atlantic Airlines, starting in 1984, Virgin Megastores in 1986 and Virgin Radio in 1993. Consequently, Robert and I led the KPMG worldwide team of accounting, tax and acquisition services for Richard's rapidly expanding Virgin Group of Companies, which, at the time, included nearly twenty companies. Most of the companies were start-up companies, and Richard astutely spent considerable time working out their potential plusses and minuses before deciding to invest. Each of the companies were owned individually such that if one business failed, it could be quietly closed down, all creditors paid, and there was no direct impact on any other Virgin Group company. This strategy worked very successfully for the following fifteen years until I left KPMG.

Since then, Richard and the Virgin Group has continued to expand his empire frequently with, at the time of writing, great interest in Virgin Galactic. This company has now completed its first fully crewed spaceflight and is planning more space travel in the future. Richard continues to still go from strength to strength, and I will always remember working with him and Robert as something really special.

Joining and Working with Film, Television and Radio Trade Organisations

If one wishes to accumulate clients in a particular industry, it is important to join as a member and participate in the activities of trade organisations that are amongst the leaders widely recognised in their relative industries.

Given KPMG's substantial share in providing accounting and consulting services, with a majority by value of media and entertainment companies in the United Kingdom and worldwide, it was deemed beneficial to spend time at industry events and meet participants. This enhanced our reputation as being competent in overall industry knowledge and, effectively, resulted in accumulating more clients in the industry.

Several reputable industry organisations participate in relevant industry events in order to raise monies for their activities and expand their membership. I attended several of these events and gleaned a substantial amount of broadcasting knowledge.

British Academy for Film and Television Arts (BAFTA)
Having a strong reputation in the UK film and television industry, leading to achieving market share of external financial services by a considerable margin; therefore, it was straightforward for me to initiate KPMG becoming a corporate member of BAFTA in Piccadilly, Central London.

This gave me and my fellow media and entertainment partners the opportunity to entertain clients and potential clients for meetings and meals at BAFTA and to hire the private cinema, showing screenings of feature films, several prior to their public release.

The Radio Academy
Before I became the head of KPMG's media and entertainment practice, the firm had accumulated a significant number of

the UK's commercial radio stations with a majority by overall turnover. I personally dealt with Heart Radio in London owned by the Chrysalis Group.

To assist in providing professional consulting services, I recruited the administrative head of the Radio Academy, whose members were virtually all of the UK's radio broadcasters, and we built a specialist team of financial advisors.

Shortly afterwards, the BBC sought bids from accountants and consultants for their audit and financial advisory services. I assisted in putting together a team that was not involved in other broadcasters and was delighted when KPMG were awarded the contract.

Then, to my surprise, I was awarded a Fellowship of the Radio Academy and have attended several midweek evening gatherings since then to keep in touch with the industry.

The Royal Television Society (RTS)

As KPMG had such a significant share of professional financial services provided to all broadcasters in the television industry as above, I became a member of the RTS over thirty years ago and still remain as such today. Attending, listening and contributing to discussions with speakers on numerous periodic gatherings was very useful in showing an increasing number of clients that we had a serious interest in their industry. When financial work was put out to tender, this was a major consideration and much additional work resulted.

Independent Programme Producers Association (IPPA)

IPPA was set up to act as producers of feature films, television, animation, children's and digital media. Over many years, the number of independent programme producers expanded substantially as it was mandated that a certain proportion of television programmes should not be produced by television companies but instead by independent producers. IPPA was formed as a trade organisation representing the members who would produce the programmes for broadcasting companies. Some of the companies awarded to produce these programmes have grown into sizeable businesses. Similar to the above, several of the larger producers employed KPMG as their financial advisors.

I subsequently recruited the chief executive of IPPA, the late Paul Styles, to work for KPMG's media and entertainment practice, adding valuable industry client knowledge to our existing media and entertainment consultancy practice. Later, he was awarded an Order of the British Empire (OBE).

Producers Alliance For Cinema And Television (PACT)
PACT is a trade association for independent producers working in feature films, television programmes, animation and digital media. As with the above, we were keen supporters of the association and assisted many of the members in dealing with the current state and issues facing them and the industry.

The combinations of the above organisations demonstrated that we were seriously keen to keep in touch with industry events and the personnel involved in the various organisations.

Working For and With Significant Charities

Huge numbers of people in the United Kingdom have contributed cash donations each year to a national or local charity and often several other worthy causes.

If they can afford it, many donors give a certain amount of their income to what they consider to be worthy causes, and this can frequently attract some income tax relief. Several of the more wealthy give substantial amounts to their favourite charities. Often, it is a lot easier to spend the short time to make a donation when a time commitment to a charitable organisation is not feasible in their personal circumstances. Time spent by donors on charities is often limited and far less easy.

I have been fortunate – together with great support, at times, from my family and my employers – to have been in a position to spend considerable time on general management and/or fundraising initiatives where specific results were noticeable.

Comic Relief
Comic Relief was founded in 1985, primarily by Richard Curtis and Lenny Henry. (Please forgive me for not mentioning the several others.) It had its first inaugural fundraising event at the Shaftesbury Theatre in 1986. The second event was the first one broadcast by the BBC in 1988 and raised the amazing sum of £15 million, followed by £27 million the following year.

In 1990, (now, Sir) Lenny Henry invited me to a breakfast meeting in the foyer at the Hilton Hotel in Shepherds Bush when he informed me that the previous accountancy firm acting as receipts treasurers felt they had done their bit, particularly as Comic Relief did not wish to pay any fees to them for the large amount of time spent collecting and banking all the numerous and prolific generous public donations. The organising company, Charity Projects Limited, had a clear ambition to avoid all costs and overheads, if remotely possible, and were keen on having public donations virtually retained totally to maximise the charitable aims of the charity. Much of the staff were on the payrolls of other entities. Two-thirds of the funds raised were planned for poorer countries in Africa.

After consultation with my senior partners, who were happy to agree, I accepted the collection role, for Comic Relief, on behalf of KPMG, with no fees or charges. This was quite timely as Peat, Marwick, Mitchell & Co., which I had joined in 1968 and became a London partner in 1987, had recently merged with Thomson McLintock to become KPMG Peat Marwick McLintock, and, in October 1991, was becoming KPMG Peat Marwick (now KPMG). For this name to be freely advertised across bumper television audiences for several hours stating where to send in donations for Red Nose Days was a huge bonus. Moreover, the collection work was mainly in the summer when monthly workloads slackened after dealing with all the December year-end audits. It also appeared attractive to numerous university graduates who would join the firm in September each year when accountancy firms had earlier been barred from publicly advertising their services as it was previously deemed unprofessional. It also helped classify KPMG as a caring firm, different from the other large firms of accountants and financial consultants, who were also competing to recruit the best university talent.

KPMG collected £87 million under my supervision and passed directly through to Comic Relief with no deductions in the next four biennial Red Nose Days resulting from the BBC-televised Friday night programmes. Having the free roam of the BBC Studio throughout the evening was also something special.

At the time of writing, Comic Relief has now raised approximately £1.5 billion for its great cause.

The Film and Television Charity (FTC), which was The Cinema and Television Benevolent Fund (CTBF), and the British Cinema and Television Veterans

Having been appointed head of KPMG's London, UK, European and Worldwide Media and Entertainment Practice in 1984, it was natural that I was asked to take over as the partner in charge of the audit and advisory services that KPMG provided to the Cinema and Television Benevolent Fund. The CTBF had then been in existence for some sixty years, designed to be the UK charity for people in need, who were working, or had worked, behind the camera in the film, cinema and commercial television industries for numerous years. It regularly and consistently has spent a welfare expenditure budget exceeding £1 million per year for many decades.

The CTBF had been established in 1924 by Lord J Arthur Rank (who founded the Rank Organisation Group) and Lord Cecil Bernstein (who founded the Granada Television Group) and they, together with other businesses and individuals in the UK film industry, also made significant donations to the CTBF. In its film and television group, the Rank Organisation Group included Pinewood and Denham Studios, Rank Film Laboratories, Rank Film Distributors, Rank Screen Advertising and Odeon Cinemas. I was appointed as the KPMG audit and advisory partner on all of the above companies in 1984 and subsequently visited their premises at least annually and sometimes more frequently than that. KPMG were also auditors and financial advisors to the Granada Group, Yorkshire Television and London Weekend Television (LWT), making up three of the big five commercial UK television channels in the UK. In 1984, I was appointed as the KPMG audit and advisory partner for LWT.

Granada and Yorkshire were two of the biggest five of the regional ITV companies in the UK and held the commercial television licences for the North West and North East of England, respectively. They were famous for decades, producing the everlasting *Coronation Street* and *Emmerdale* "soap" programmes, which are still being broadcast on ITV several times each week. As a side effect, similar to the Rank Organisation, the CTBF was potentially very useful to them and the whole of their industry to the extent that, if a current or former employee was in hardship, there was the potential availability of external help and subsistence from the charity. The employee only needed to have worked in the industry for a few years before being considered for benefits.

The charity has always been blessed with Royal patronage, mainly headed by the late HM The Queen and HRH The Duke of Edinburgh, who attended regular Royal Film Performances for decades, sometimes represented in more recent years by HRH Prince Charles (now King Charles) and the Duchess of Cornwall (now Queen Camilla). For the first time in 2020, HRH The Duke and Duchess of Cambridge attended the recent premiere of the latest James Bond film. More details of my close involvement with members of the Royal Family are included in the 'Working Personally with Royalty' chapter.

For numerous decades, KPMG were the external auditors and financial advisors of the Stock Exchange-listed companies of the Rank Organisation and its subsidiaries and also the Granada Group were the natural choice to act as the charity's auditors and financial advisors. This was further enhanced because members of the Peat family (the founders of KPMG) had acted as financial advisors to the Royal Family for decades.

Also, for numerous decades, the CTBF owned and operated a retirement-care home called Glebelands in Wokingham, Berkshire, as well as assisting numerous potential industry beneficiaries with cash grants across the UK. As a member and subsequent chairman of the Finance and Estates Committee after I left KPMG in 2000, I was closely involved in selling the spare land near the entrance to the home for £4 million. Whilst president, I was also heavily involved in the expansion of the retirement facility by building flats as an extension to the retirement home, named the "Broccoli Cloisters". This was thought appropriate as the charity had received a £1million donation from the family of the late "Cubby" Broccoli, who, together with his family, have produced all the unbelievably successful James Bond films and supported the charity to a considerable extent for decades to date. I was also heavily involved, some years later, with the sale of Glebelands to Anchor Homes to continue the good work nationwide. The CTBF then had more funds to finance spaces at other retirement and care homes available across the UK and to embark, in more recent years. on providing important care services to UK employees in the media and entertainment industry in their time of need.

Shortly after leaving KPMG in 2000, after being one of the members of its International Board for more than a decade (latterly holding two different roles at the same time as Worldwide Head of both Marketing and the Worldwide Media and Entertainment Practices in the firm), I joined the Finance and Investment Committee of the CTBF, subsequently becoming chairman and was elected to the Board of Trustees shortly afterwards. I subsequently became deputy president of the charity in 2005 and was president for three years from 2008.

At the biennial Royal Film Performances at the Odeon Cinema in Leicester Square, as the then-president and subsequently immediate past-president, I was required to greet the Patron HM The Queen, HRH The Duke of Edinburgh or, in some years, the then-HRH Prince Charles and the then-HRH the Duchess of Cornwall in the foyer and introduce them to the line-up of trustees of the CTBF and a few beneficiaries. This is expanded upon in the chapter about personally working with numerous members of the Royal Family.

I stepped down from the Board of Trustees in 2016 after thirty-two years of close involvement and was appointed as a vice patron and remain so up to now. I remained on the Finance and Investment Committee until 2020. The charity has consistently had some £20 million of reserve funds placed with the investment management bank, N. M. Rothschild & Co. Amazingly, and to its great credit, Rothschild has consistently produced investment gains of £1.5 million per year, roughly equal to the otherwise unfunded annual welfare and other expenditure up to very recent years ago. An amazing achievement consistently performed.

During my time as president of the charity, a further amazing event resulted when, unfortunately, Peter Rogers – the producer of the *Carry On* series of films, and whose wife produced the *Doctor* series of films – died in 2009. His wife, Betty Box, had pre-deceased him (1999), the pair had no children, and he had specifically disinherited a nephew. In his will, he basically left everything to the Cinema and Television Benevolent Fund, including his house and the ownership of his company, Peter Rogers Productions Limited. Amazingly, for more than a decade, now, after his death, the company has consistently made profits of between £200,000 and £300,000 per year in total from ITV for the UK rights and Canal Plus for the overseas rights. It was expected that these royalties would decline over a period, but this has not happened until maybe recently as there has invariably been about a quarter of a million UK viewers watching one of these films on numerous Saturday mornings and other times during the year. What Rogers did was one of the all-time great bequests by anybody.

Now, recently renamed the Film and Television Charity (FTC), it continues to exist to support creatives, production professionals, marketeers and administration staff from script to screen who find themselves in times of hardship. The only exceptions for beneficiaries in the UK, across the whole of the film and television industry, are actors and actresses and personnel, who have their own charity, and those who worked solely for the BBC, who have their own benevolent fund arrangements.

In recent years, I was voted in as a member of the British Cinema and Television Veterans and, in 2022, was voted on to the Executive Committee. One of the benefits to the veterans is unlimited free admission to numerous cinemas for afternoon screenings.

It has been a pleasure to work with all the Board members of both organisations continuously for nearly forty years.

Working Personally with Royalty

There is a huge number of citizens, in the UK and worldwide, who admire and respect the UK's royal family. Many of the Royals do great work on so many days each year.

It has been my privilege to have worked with many of them on several occasions, mainly to enhance charities and good causes. As mentioned in the charities section of this book, I was closely and continuously involved for thirty-four years, from 1984 to 2018, working, initially, on a part-time basis, as the external auditor and, latterly, as the president/trustee of the Cinema and Television Benevolent Fund, now renamed the Film and Television Charity. This charity has always been grateful to receive the patronage of His Majesty King Charles and the late Her Majesty The Queen and their partners who have attended, prior to the national release of numerous perennial Royal Film Performances, generally at the Odeon Leicester Square in London. This has, in total, earned many millions of pounds for this worthy charity. This included several James Bond film premieres, thanks to the Broccoli family who have been huge supporters of the charity.

Whilst I was appointed the president and then, subsequently, the former president of the charity totalling six consecutive years in the early part of this century, it was my pleasure to welcome the royals in the foyer, following the seating of all other attendees, Her Majesty the Queen and the Duke of Edinburgh, and, on one occasion, now-King Charles and now-Queen Camilla into the foyer of the Odeon Leicester Square to introduce them to my fellow Trustees, their partners and some of the charity's beneficiaries.

At the time, it was quite daunting to need to remember all of the names of the many people in the line-up, even though I knew many of them very well. With my wife, I would sit next to the Royals during the film and make sure they were comfortable. As several people know, I am well capable of falling asleep at some stages of watching a film, but I always managed to stay awake when the Royals were so close. The Duke and the King were always amusing and entertaining; as an example, the Duke quite often queried, 'Why did an actor commit a crime when he was bound to be caught?'! They were so natural and went to great lengths to put people at ease.

At the end of the performance, it was necessary for me to see them safely into their car returning them to Buckingham Palace before the audience were able to leave the cinema. It has been my privilege to have worked with many of the Royal Family on those occasions, mainly to enhance the charities and good causes.

In the years during my presidency, the charity agreed to set up the John Brabourne Awards. He was a close relative of Her Majesty the Queen and produced several films, including *A Passage to India*. The plan was to periodically donate £5,000 to assist a limited number of young potential film scriptwriters to help finance them during the time needed to write the necessary scripts. For many years, up to the start of this century, a Cinema and Television Benevolent Fund Committee was appointed to adjudicate on the successful authors.

After a while, a number of candidates had qualified for their awards, and it was decided that the awards should be acknowledged at a special evening dinner at BAFTA in Piccadilly. I was familiar with the venue as I had initiated corporate membership for KPMG some years earlier.

As she was the president of BAFTA, the Princess Royal heard of the event and informed me that she wished to attend and support it. As the most senior trustee of the charity present, I and my wife sat next to her for the dinner before introducing her to do the prizegiving. She works so hard and had attended six different events in the Midlands on that day before returning to London by helicopter. We recalled the time that I had initiated KPMG as a corporate member of BAFTA and the special screenings we had held in their premises, inviting key clients and contacts to their private theatre in Piccadilly in earlier years. We also remembered travelling to Los Angeles to incorporate the newly formed United States BAFTA. This coincided with my annual visit, as the head of KPMG's Worldwide Media and Entertainment practice, to Los Angeles to attend the American Film Market and to see the local specialist KPMG media and entertainment partners in their Hollywood offices and to see local clients. The Princess was so easy to talk to, and it was evident that she puts in the work for her royal duties and charities.

Prince Edward had set up his own production company, Ardent, and on behalf of KPMG, I invited him to lunch on our hired boat in Cannes harbour at the international television marketing event, called Marché International des Programmes de Communication (MIPCOM), in the late 1990s, where, as with all of us, he met a lot of key contacts in the worldwide television industry.

MIPCOM is where television executives from all over the world meet annually in October each year, marketing their upcoming productions. On the following day, whilst on the gangplank welcoming different lunch guests for the second day, I noticed Prince Edward and his chief executive were walking along the jetty enjoying the scenery. I went down the gangplank to inquire if the market was proving helpful to them, to which they said that it was. I asked if they had any lunch arrangements, and they said no. I said that they were welcome on our boat again, but this was initially turned down as they did not have a written invitation! I said that was not necessary and was pleased to have them join us even if we were not observing protocols.

Working on Live Pop Tours

People quite often imagine that chartered accountants sit in their office from 9 am to 5 pm five days every week, adding up numbers, except for a few weeks' holiday. However, many of my assignments were not done sitting in my London office. One of the best assignments in my career was carried out for Prince Rupert Loewenstein and his colleagues. He was the head of the UK private bank, called Leopold Joseph. Amongst many other clients at the bank, he was the financial manager for the Rolling Stones and Pink Floyd bands.

When it came to the bands' worldwide tours, it was easy to find out the numbers of how many people were attending the arenas as each venues' number of seats was easily verifiable. Plus, it was not difficult to calculate how much the promoter had raised, based on the number of admissions for a full attendance and how much was due to the band, based on the signed contract.

However, when it came to outdoor venues, how could the number of the tens of thousands of attendees be easily verified and, consequently, based on the number of attendees, how much the promoter would have received and how much did he have to pay the band. The contract with the promoter would have a base minimum figure to pay for a substantial audience but with an overage, due to the band, on the numbers attending over the minimum figure.

It was a regular occurrence that one or more of the turnstiles at the venues would be out of order, and so it was impossible to know exactly how many people had passed through that turnstile and, therefore, the total number attending the gig.

I was in charge of my colleagues checking the number of attendees at the Rolling Stones performance at Wembley Stadium and had access to all areas, to seek to agree with the promoter on the night how many people had attended. It could go long into the night before an agreement was reached, but the rules of the game were that nobody could go home until the relevant number was agreed upon. Often this went on through many hours into the night after the performance was over.

Settlement of the consequential financial figures based on the agreed number of attendees would be sorted out in later days. My KPMG colleagues dealt with the same attendance situation on all the overseas performances of the two bands in various arenas.

After I left KPMG, the Rolling Stones played live in the middle of Rio de Janeiro, and I suspect there had to be a fixed fee for the performance, as how could anybody be precise about the number of people who were there?

Leasing Hundreds of Cars

An amazing experience happened across the whole of the United Kingdom in the 1990s when HM Government implemented a national pay freeze due to the then-exceptionally rampant rate of inflation in employees' salaries and the general cost of living. This limitation applied to basic salaries for executives but did not apply to employee benefits. The KPMG partners in London and the South East of England made the decision, in addition to paying static basic salaries, to lease and pay for three years of monthly contracts to provide a family saloon car for senior and junior departmental managers up to a reasonable, but controlled, amount. This was effectively a pay increase but complied with the law. After three years, the car was returned to the leasing company and replaced with another one.

Originally, this business was placed with Interleasing, deliberately not a client of KPMG to avoid potential allegations of a lack of independence with financial services clients, of which KPMG had one of, if not, *the* highest number of any accounting firm. However, as the number of leased cars rose substantially and quickly, clients, like National Westminster Bank, complained that their leasing subsidiary, Lex, should be allowed to compete. As there was fair competition amongst all the leasing companies, this was granted as there was no favouritism. This was subsequently extended to include other clients of the firm.

With a simple pack of information, every manager was entitled to choose a reasonable, but not extravagant, saloon car and leasing company of their choice up to a defined limit. Each was also allowed to go up to twenty per cent over the limit paid for by the firm, and this excess was equalised by a salary sacrifice for the difference. Due to its simplicity and a guide book of instructions, it was easy for my personal assistant to manage the clearly defined process of dealing with leasing each car, and I only needed to confirm the monthly bills received were correct.

Within a short number of years, the number of cars (and different leasing companies) rocketed into many hundreds with different suppliers. As the partner in charge of the programme, even with the process mainly totally virtually delegated to administrative staff on a day-to-day basis, each of the leasing companies offered me numerous free invitations to a wide range of sporting and numerous other high quality events, many of the sporting kind. With a full client list of mainly media and entertainment companies and other KPMG partnership responsibilities on worldwide activities, it was impossible for me to fit many of them in. However, out of the best invitations, several of the evening events were possible as was one of the big invitations to play golf with professionals in Germany on the European Golf Tour, which is in the Golf chapter of this book.

Thirty years later, there are still some golf and other reunions each year for former clients of the car-leasing companies.

Worldwide Marketing of a Leading Professional Services Firm

When one mentions you are head of Worldwide Marketing for a large worldwide professional services firm, eyebrows raise as to how does one do that, assuming people are interested. People understand businesses that have a tangible product. They often are aware of the quality and competitive pricing of various products and why owners wish to promote it. Often, they can visualise the product and, on observation or by enquiry with others about its qualities, they can decide whether they wish to buy or not.

But what about professional services firms, and how does one firm of accountants, solicitors or other professional firms differentiate itself from another when a number of firms appear to be offering similar services, and, arguably, there is often not a huge difference between the merits of the larger firms. Like banks, it is not easy for individuals to be certain which is the best bank in the country at which to open an account.

Up until several decades ago, accounting and other professional services firms did not overtly advertise as it was then often considered to be an unprofessional thing to do. Accountancy firms occasionally would be named publicly more widely when dealing with insolvencies or occasional television news programmes commenting on a then-current financial issue of considerable significance to numerous businesses or individuals. For example, Peat, Marwick, Mitchell & Co. (PMM now KPMG) received numerous public mentions when they were appointed as the receivers of Rolls Royce in 1971, three years after I joined their London office as a newly qualified chartered accountant. There was widespread public and business interest due to the high quality of the brand, and it was of great interest to many, hoping that the business could survive (which it did and has), limiting the number of the many jobs that would otherwise be lost.

Gradually over the years, the original Big Eight accounting firms were reduced by mergers some decades later to a Big Four. This was when PMM worldwide merged with another accounting firm, Thomson McLintock. They came to be more in the public domain and were regarded as commercial businesses. Coherent plans between the numerous KPMG firms around the world were developed and had a strong international board, which I joined. This oversaw the expansion in over fifty countries.

Two specialist industry groups at KPMG had always been strong with acknowledged specialists in the banking and insurance services industries, but a substantial number of their other staff worked in numerous general practice departments of about thirty qualified and trainee chartered accountants. When the number of industry specialist departments and partners expanded, I became the partner in charge of the newly created UK's media and entertainment practice and subsequently became the head of KPMG's European and Worldwide Media and Entertainment Practices operating in numerous tens of countries. This was as well as head of Worldwide Marketing sitting on the Worldwide Board, a virtually unique situation holding two of the less than twenty positions on the board at the same time. This involved many responsibilities involving enhancing the above and making sure there was consistent high-quality service throughout the KPMG firms around the world. Amongst many of the countries I visited, this included four visits to Cannes each year at the international markets promoting KPMG's music, television and film practices, as set out below.

In January and April each year for a decade, from 1990 to 2000, on behalf of KPMG, I and my colleagues took a stand at the two separate worldwide music and television industry events in the Palais in Cannes. This was supported by KPMG's other media and entertainment specialists from several other countries. A huge proportion of the world's leading music, television and film industry companies attended the event, and it demonstrated that KPMG was seriously interested in, almost exclusively, specialists in the industries. Numerous constructive conversations were held with those visitors and other exhibitors. In the following months, valuable new business was obtained worldwide, stemming from those meetings, distinguishing KPMG from other professional services firms who were not there or did not specialise.

Several people wondered what KPMG would put on the television monitor positioned on each stand at the above events for several days. Obviously, we were not marketing a television programme or a music item, so what could we do? At home, I had recorded a copy of some fifty sporting cock-up clips shown by the BBC on its *Sports Reviews of the Year,* held in late December for several years. The best and relatively famous clip is when the man at the back of the bobsleigh pushes the sleigh to start the downhill run. When he has it moving, he invariably jumps in to join the passenger but, on this occasion, he slips and falls and does not board the sleigh speeding off down the steep run. People are left to guess what eventually happened farther down the run. The BBC had noted that, thankfully and amazingly, nobody was hurt by the runaway bobsleigh. Being interested as to what would happen next, visitors to Cannes would then stop and speak to us and afterwards and pick up one of the brochures showing KPMG services to international media and entertainment businesses. In October, my colleagues and I would visit the second international television event for the conversations with leading worldwide television companies. We would charter a boat on the quay in Cannes and host a large lunch for clients and industry contacts.

Every May, I would visit the Cannes film festival solely to mix with film executives all over the world but virtually all of the business activity was outside the Palais, and we did not formally exhibit, although I had several good meetings.

As head of KPMG's Worldwide Media and Entertainment Practice as well as head of Worldwide Marketing, each with multi-million budgets, I was required to attend quarterly meetings of the KPMG Worldwide Board. These were never in the United States or Europe but in numerous other places, like Brisbane.

One of my most memorable moments was flying from London to Brisbane and sleeping overnight on the plane. When I woke up at 7 am Brisbane time on a Saturday morning, I noticed that virtually all of the ten planes on the ground were JAL Japanese jumbo jets. For a moment, I thought I might have got on the wrong plane and had arrived in Tokyo, but on enquiry from the flight attendant, she said they were the planes bringing the Japanese golfers in to play weekend golf in Eastern Australia. On finishing work on the Friday evening, they would fly overnight to Brisbane, arrive on the Saturday morning, play golf later on Saturday and again on Sunday morning, and then fly back to Tokyo in time to go to work on Monday morning. Due to Japan being seventy per cent mountainous, there are very few golf courses there, and most golfers attend only indoor driving ranges. This was an expensive alternative to play their sport.

Upon becoming head of KPMG's Worldwide Marketing Department, I worked on a review of how all the various countries and continents carried out their marketing. The first and obvious plan was to harmonise and make consistent all the promotional activity worldwide. All colours, layouts and messages in the brochures were to be made consistent, and all countries were building on the best practices identified worldwide. This had a significant boost to how each individual country would grow.

Travel to numerous countries resulted in KPMG's share of clients in the worldwide media and entertainment industries increasing significantly to a level above any other accounting and financial consulting firm.

Product Placement and Advertising Professional Firm

Before being informed of the unusual commercial advertising process of product placement, I had never really ever been made aware of what was involved and why it should ever be considered. Moreover, I found out that many of the people I knew also did not know much about it either, mainly due to its subtlety.

When I was the partner at KPMG responsible for worldwide marketing, I decided to pay one-off fees to incorporate the firm's name into the scripts of more than a dozen feature films and popular television programmes. It was not many years earlier that it had become permissible for accountancy firms to advertise. As an example, a repeat of one of the long-running series of the *Heartbeat* programmes incorporating the KPMG name is still being shown on ITV some twenty-five years later after first screenings.

As a typical example, in one feature film, when a business was suffering financially, and clearly its management needed financial assistance to survive, the original script was set to say, 'You need to get some financial advice and assistance to improve your business so that you can continue to trade and prosper. Otherwise, you are going to face insolvency'. Adding the words, 'I think you should take some advice from some reputable financial advisors, like KPMG, and they should be able to help you resolve your problem'. This fitted in with the original script and was popular with film and television producers who thought it enhanced the realism of the script, and they received extra monies.

Another example was when an individual, who is known to need to be seeking financial advice or assistance, is seen walking into a building with its exterior and the KPMG logo temporarily, but clearly, shown on-screen. The sign was possibly on the building for only a few hours but was long enough for the letters to be photographed whilst the film or commercial television programme was being recorded (e.g., made/created). It was very subtle, but many buildings have company names written on their exteriors.

These programmes also subtly appeared on BBC television programmes, particularly when showing feature films. This bypassed the corporation's "No Advertising" policy but thankfully, no complaints ever materialised.

Many UK television programmes and feature films were shown in numerous countries, so the exposure worldwide was significant where KPMG had local offices.

I thought it possible that only a very few people would notice, but I was quite surprised when several people I knew and existing clients and staff of KPMG remarked on what they had seen and been impressed and mildly amused. This was mainly about the subtlety and maybe its novelty and cheekiness. The cost in advertising terms was relatively inexpensive. Nobody ever complained.

Film producers greatly enjoyed the ploy as the inclusion of the letters made the film look more realistic, and they received some extra funds from KPMG to aid them whilst making their films.

Playing Golf Worldwide

I appreciate that there are a substantial number of people in the world who consider the sport of golf as being boring, a waste of time and a waste of a good walk for hitting and chasing after a tiny ball and trying to get it into a little hole, maybe up to a quarter of a mile away or so. However, this chapter deals with many magical or other moments played and/or organised and experienced by me on various golf courses around the world in the last six decades, some of which are still current today in 2024. I have greatly enjoyed playing in five continents in the world and made many additional friends in so doing.

When I was the head of Worldwide Marketing and holding two positions, simultaneously, on the KPMG International Board of twenty members or so in the late 1990s, the Japanese KPMG practice said they would not approve of paying their share of any of the dozen or so international KPMG budgets that were paid for by some 100 countries in the world based on their relative fee incomes. This view would change only if KPMG sponsored a well-known international golfer that would be appreciated by their golf-playing clients as seen by them on Japanese television and worldwide. Given my position as a keen golfer and with virtually no others on the International Board playing golf, I was requested to rectify the situation as best as possible. At the time, there were only three of the top twenty golfers in the world available for such a sponsorship, and not all of the very talented players available had reputations deemed by all to be suitable for such a sponsorship by a leading professional services firm.

Luckily, at the time, the star man, who was potentially available was the very high quality and greatly admired-for-decades-United-States player, Phil Mickelson. I commenced discussions with his manager, leading to the agreement of KPMG sponsoring Phil. Amazingly, for more than twenty years, until recently, he has worn those four letters on his cap every time he plays in tournaments around the world, except when he has played every four years for his country against Europe in the Ryder Cup and against other countries' professional golfers in the Presidents Cup matches. This is when he has worn "USA" on his cap, like all his fellow team players. The KPMG contract has clearly and visibly been renewed several times during the last twenty-plus years or so since I left the firm in 2000. The letters have featured on worldwide golf television programmes for up to four continuous days each time he plays in over thirty four-day tournaments around the world every year. We believe the letters have been seen in well over fifty countries.

It has been publicly reported that his earnings on the United States Golf Tour have recently topped US $92 million, second only to Tiger Woods. Phil has also featured in forty-five individual matches, playing for the US Team against the European team in the Ryder Cup, which occurred every four years. Amazingly, at his age, he won the United States Open Golf Tournament in 2021, one of the Big Four professional golf tournaments in the world.

However, in 2021, Phil's contract with KPMG was cancelled as he had joined the Saudi Arabian-backed LIV international tour, a rival tour to the US and European tours. So, it was helpful that I had previously signed to begin the KPMG sponsorship of the very amiable Irishman, Ronan Rafferty, to wear KPMG logos on his cap, for a number of years, whilst on the European Golf Tour. I had also signed the late Malcolm Gregson to do the same on the European Seniors (older than their 50s) Golf Tour. These were three wonderful and very good-natured ambassadors for KPMG for decades, wherever they appeared and featured on television for a considerable number of days in numerous countries for many years. During their sponsorships, they were happy to host client golf days in the country that they were about to play the tournaments, and this was considered an exceptional and special invitation to golf-playing executives at key KPMG clients.

Early Days of Playing

There are few discussions on subjects in the world where opinions are more divisive than when mentioning the word "golf". Many wonder why so many golfers in so many countries in the world "waste" time and money for, say, four to five hours at one time nonstop consistently attempting to put a little ball into a very small hole, say, about a quarter of a mile away for each of the eighteen holes. Critics fail to realise all the health and fitness benefits of walking with friends about five miles per full round of golf in fresh air. They also fail to appreciate the challenge of competition between golfers in a worldwide sport, often taking place amongst beautiful scenery often seen only by many golfers, on private (competition) property. Neither do they understand the unique handicapping system, which means that, on a good day, a poorer golfer can beat a better golfer on any course and even amateurs could possibly defeat professional players who have a handicap of zero. For example, on a usual eighteen-hole golf course, if a golfer has a handicap of, say, eighteen, he or she starts with a one-shot advantage on each hole over his fellow competitors with a zero handicap, like a professional golfer. The better golfer, therefore, has to play two shots less, not one, in order to win a hole. This is a classic case of levelling up all players.

I first started to play golf at the age of 12 years at West Somerset Golf Club in Minehead, Somerset, playing in school holidays against a school friend of similar age. It was a lovely seaside course overlooking the Bristol Channel and South Wales, close to where the Butlin's holiday complex is now situated. We would not play so much in the winter but would usually play more than once a week at other times in school holidays each year except when we were on holidays with our parents. We were approximately of the same ability and had some good games with the golf, itself, being mildly competitive.

Like many other golf courses, it was quite easy, if desired, to shorten the distance and the time played on any one day as many of the first nine holes went in one direction from the clubhouse with the second nine holes mainly coming back by the seaside. It was, therefore, easy to play, for example, the first and last six holes, shortening the amount of walking and playing time spent, by a third, if desired.

My mother, father and I, and in earlier years with my middle brother, used to hire clubs and play a nine-hole golf course in Jersey for some days every year on our annual holiday there when I was between 11 and 16 years of age. Every Thursday in the summer, the various localities in Jersey took turns having their individual "fetes" for the year, with fresh produce and locally made items on sale. At the time, in the latter part of the day, people would play a dice game, called *Crown and Anchor*, on a betting table. I believe this was played in the Navy, but, at the time, it was illegal in England.

The six sides of the dice had pictures of a heart, a club, a diamond and a spade, as well as a crown and an anchor. The croupier would throw three dice. If the dice came up with three different items, he would pay out even money on the three revealed and collect off the other three that were not. If two of one item came up, he would pay out two to one on the two and one to one on the other, totalling three payouts, but he would collect off four. If the dice came up with three of a kind, he would pay out three to one and collect off five.

The croupier was, therefore, keen that the three dice were not all different. In the first year, I believe my father won all or almost the whole cost of the holiday on one evening. Not surprisingly, he wanted to and did go back to Jersey for several future years to repeat his success, but I am fairly certain he never did. It was his one-off fun for the year. He enjoyed the challenge and never bet a lot.

However, the total amount of golf I played was reduced, and my handicap of sixteen increased after I left Taunton School at almost 16 years of age and commenced my five-year full-time training at the local chartered accountancy firm of Amherst & Shapland in Minehead, passing all the examinations to become a Chartered Accountant in 1967. At 21 years old, this was the earliest age to achieve this qualification. In later years, it became almost mandatory to go to university after taking A-level examinations and, therefore, the earliest age of qualification rose to about 24 years old, with the training time reduced from five years to three.

I left Minehead in 1968 soon after qualification for what was intended to be three years' invaluable work experience in London with Peat, Marwick, Mitchell & Co. (now KPMG), one of the biggest accounting and financial consulting firms in the world. However, due to unanticipated promotions, mentioned elsewhere in this book, rising to holding two positions at the same time on the KPMG Worldwide International Board and taking up subsequent major directorships after I left KPMG in 2000, whilst I visited Minehead frequently to start with, I never returned to Somerset to live or play golf.

Middle-Age Days

Whilst pursuing an unexpectedly lengthy international career with Peat, Marwick, Mitchell &Co/KPMG, often working away from home for considerable periods, sometimes overseas, it meant that the time needed for golf was really not desirable, available or fair to my family, and golf, therefore, became a rare activity. I did join West Hill Golf Club, near Woking, for a short while, but gave it up as a member when the expense outweighed the time available to play there, and I moved away from the area. I then joined Silvermere Golf & Leisure (near Weybridge/Walton on Thames) as an occasional pay-and-play member as the golf I was playing was on odd days and not regularly at one place. Silvermere offers a sixty-four-booth driving range (said to be the biggest in Europe) and numerous professionals giving lessons, plus the complex has the biggest professional shop in England, selling golf clothing, clubs and other golf accessories.

However, there *were* matches, often annual, between KPMG personnel and some KPMG clients of mine, and the match against the investment bankers of N. M. Rothschild & Co was always a big joust and very competitive. This was similar for the matches played against other clients: London Weekend Television (operators of the ITV London Studios on London's South Bank), and Stephenson Harwood (solicitors to the KPMG London partnership).

In 1971, I first played at the very private Swinley Forest Golf Club at Ascot on the second Tuesday in March with the Old Tauntonian Golf Society, the alumni of Taunton School in Somerset. Like West Hill, this is ranked in the very top echelons of golf courses in England. It is extremely difficult for any golfer to play there unless invited by a society or by one of the limited number of members, and every player needs permission from the club. The scenery is stunning near Sunningdale in Ascot, and every hole is completely different. I took over the organisation of this annual event some twenty years ago and have now completed the fifty-second year of my attendance with about forty golfers playing each year. The whole ambience of the course, scenery, peace, the charming clubhouse and its excellent lunches and personnel are always really special.

Three outstanding and amazing experiences happened in consecutive years in June 1996, 1997 and 1998. Earlier in the 1990s, in the UK, there had been a national pay freeze of basic salaries to seek to control the rampant rate of inflation and cost of living. Surprisingly, this restriction did not apply to employees' benefits. KPMG partners in the London office took the decision to offer managers a three-year, leased family car of their choice, free of charge, up to a reasonable limit. They could go twenty per cent over the limit, if they accepted a salary sacrifice for the difference. This free family car was in addition to their static salary and meant that they did not need to spend any of their basic salary to purchase one. The scheme was managed daily by my secretary under my overall guidance.

Originally, this business was placed with Interleasing, but after a considerable rise, a fair proportion of the considerable number of cars leased was placed with the then-management of Leasecontracts and other companies in later years. In the spring of 1996, as one of Leasecontracts' bigger customers, I was invited to a lunch at The Ivy's restaurant and upstairs private dining room in London. BMW's European Sales Director was at the lunch. Amazingly, he wished to invite all those present to visit Germany to play in the Pro-Am the day before the annual European Tour event, which was starting in Eichenreid on 19 June 1996. On the day before the event, we would be picked up at our homes in the morning, to fly out and arrive on time for the draw in the evening of who would play with each European Tour professional the following day. I was provided with free air tickets, transportation in Germany and excellent hospitality throughout courtesy of BMW, for which I was duly grateful.

I teed off in a competition of 168 players on 19 June 1996 having drawn, the evening before, to play in a four-ball with Ronan Rafferty, the legendary professional Irish and Ryder Cup player, and two other Leasecontracts clients. The best score out of the four of us for each hole would be the only score recorded for the hole. After handicap adjustment, I would receive one shot per hole, when compared to par and Ronan's score. On the 220-yard 16th hole, I hit my ball about 35 yards short of the green, followed by Ronan hitting an outstanding tee shot to within two feet of the hole. As there was cut fairway all the way to the green and the hole, and although there was a slight uphill gradient, I decided to putt the ball. Ronan advised that I might be better to chip the ball onto the green. I understood the request, but in the circumstances of where Ronan's ball was, I/we had nothing to lose. Having learnt to play on a seaside course, with often large-cut fairways in front of the green, I putted the ball to three inches away from the hole, walked up and tapped my ball in for a net of handicap two shots and advised him to pick up his great tee shot up as it would not count and improve our team score. As stated earlier, on behalf of KPMG, I signed sponsorship terms for Ronan on the European Tour for many years afterwards. He is one of the most amiable persons I ever met.

I was invited to play in the same event in each of the following two years. I was drawn to play with Russell Claydon in 1997 and, in the following year, with the big-hitting Argentinian, Angel Cabrera. What a fantastic experience for an average British amateur golfer!

Later Days

Around the turn of the century (2000), one of the biggest customers in my two London bars and restaurants (see separate chapter) invited me to play as a guest initially, later as a member, with a golf society called the Optimists. This was a group consisting mainly of insolvency practitioners, bankers, solicitors and accountants, who were good golfers and very convivial in nature. Each year, we were teamed up to play one four-day trip each year outside England, plus a one-day event in the home counties. I joined them on several trips to Portugal, mainly in the South, plus Belgium, Scotland and France. These were great events to join in, although they were a real hammering of one's liver. In later life, I now attend the one-day Optimists event in England to keep in touch and also an outstanding Christmas lunch, which does not permit much work to be done in the afternoon!

For many years, I have been a member of the Variety Golf Society with a membership of about 100. It has numerous well-known comedians, sportsmen and other celebrities included in its membership. It has about a dozen golf fixtures each year and, at least, one annual function in a top London hotel. The latter raised the amazing sum of over £420,000 in 2021, mostly due to sponsorships and the auction of high-value items. Cumulatively, the charity raised an amazing £1.6 million in 2024. This provided a substantial number of "Sunshine Coaches", which are specially adapted mini-coaches for about twenty people, enabling handicapped children to enter via wheelchair access rising near the back of the vehicle. This means they can leave their homes and visit the seaside or other outdoor attractions for a day trip, which they would normally not be able to visit. The look of sheer happiness on the faces of the few handicapped children who would come to each presentation of the coach with their carers is unbelievably gratifying and always brings tears to my eyes.

Since 2000, and after leaving KPMG, I have become a member of the London Weekend Television (LWT) Golf Society, which has about eight one-day fixtures and an away-weekend between March and October each year in the South of England. This still has nearly thirty members, several who had worked full time in their earlier life at the London Studios on London's South Bank. This television company operated the London ITV franchise from about 6 pm on Friday evenings until midnight on Sundays. I was the partner in charge of the external audit and external advisor of London Weekend Television for virtually all twenty years of 1980 through to 2000 and was a principal advisor on their franchise renewal victory during that time.

Every second year, the fifteen regional ITV companies who then held ITV franchises had a three- or four-day golf competition hosted by a regional broadcaster that was far away from London. As LWT were short of one player in their two teams in two different years in the 1990s, I was invited to play for the believed-to-be-weaker B team twice and it was far from London. Because I was their external audit partner and was meant to be independent, I had to get special clearance from the KPMG senior partner to play in these one-off events for a client team. In the second year, I remember playing for the LWT B Golf team at North Berwick in Scotland. Little did I (or anybody else early on) realise until the very last hole that the whole multi-day event was turning on the outcome of the final singles match in which I was playing. They had put me out last hoping the event would be decided well before my match was decided so the result of my match would not matter. My match was very competitive and evenly contested. Whilst playing the last hole, I was informed that if I could put the ball on the treacherous final green with my next shot and then take no more than two putts on the treacherous final green, the

LWT B team would win the whole competition. I just about managed to do so to numerous looks of amazement and was mobbed by my team.

In later years after leaving KPMG, I joined the London Weekend Television (LWT) Golf Society and have enjoyed many happy times, playing in numerous UK locations with them.

Thirty Years Golf Tour to Jersey

In early October 1987, as a London partner in KPMG, I led three colleagues, Douglas Flint (now, Sir Douglas), who subsequently became the Group Finance Director and Group Chairman of the HSBC Holdings Banking Group; Paul George, who later became the Executive Director of the UK's Financial and Reporting Council; and Mike Roden, who became a Senior Partner in KPMG. We collectively invited 12 KPMG clients and key contacts to a two-day golfing trip to Jersey. This was to play at the very special and beautiful golf club at La Moye in the West of Jersey, which is quite private like many other golf clubs. This involved meeting early at London Gatwick Airport for breakfast before taking the fifty-minute flight to Jersey. This started an event, which ran annually over thirty-two years, except missing one year in 2012 due to exceptional circumstances. There were eighty-one different players who featured during that period. In the initial years, we stayed the night at the Portelet Hotel in Portelet Bay, but, for the later twenty years, we moved to the L'Horizon Beach Hotel & Spa in St Brelade's Bay, not far away.

Generally, on arriving in Jersey, a Tantivy thirty-seater coach would be waiting at the Jersey airport, take us to the hotel to check in and drop off our overnight bag before proceeding to the Golf Club for an early lunch. We would then play an afternoon round of golf before Tantivy would take us back to the hotel for dinner. The following morning, Tantivy would pick us up at the hotel and take us to La Moye Golf Club for the second round, followed by a late lunch and prizegiving before the transfer direct to Jersey airport to travel back home. A very busy thirty-six hours.

When arriving in Jersey for the first time with guests, it was being advertised at the airport that the evening we were going to be in Jersey was the last evening of Comedian Stan Boardman's summer season booking appearing at a club in First Tower near St Helier. I brought the dinner forward and arranged transport and tickets for us to see Stan's hilarious performance. When travelling home on the second day, we bumped into Stan at the airport, who was also on his way home. In every year after, for thirty years, we always travelled with a professional comedian, mostly through my membership of the Variety Golf Society, to be with us throughout the two days. These included, in addition to Stan, Ian Irving, Bobby Davro, Les Dennis, Duggie Brown, Aidan J Harvey, Keith O'Keefe, Dave Wolfe and Barry Took.

And, on ten occasions, I took great professional golfers with me; the late Malcolm Gregson, who I sponsored for KPMG on the European Seniors Tour, and Ronan Rafferty, who I sponsored for KPMG on the main European Tour. Also attending on a few occasions was another Variety Golf Society member, the legendary former football club manager, Dave Bassett. He managed Watford, Sheffield United, Crystal Palace, Nottingham Forest, Barnsley, Leicester and Southampton, as well as Wimbledon where he rose to fame. There was laughter throughout on the thirty-six-hour trip, and I always hired a private room for the lunches and the dinner.

The golf course at La Moye Golf Club has wonderful clifftop views with differing ones on virtually every hole. At certain places, one can see the fantastic Three-Mile Beach at St Ouen's Bay, La Corbiere Lighthouse, the North West Coast of Jersey, as well as the other Channel Islands of Guernsey, Sark and Alderney, plus the tip of Northern France. Given my family experience of Jersey, mentioned earlier in this book, the island will always hold many very special thoughts in my heart forever.

Television Appearances and the Media

Why would a chartered accountant in practice make so many television and radio appearances? And why would he be quoted in numerous daily newspapers and trade magazines on media and entertainment issues. Some people would naturally expect them to sit in their offices from 9 am to 5 pm for five days a week (except for annual holidays) adding up numbers and preparing accounts. Many confuse them as bookkeepers, sitting at the same office desk most days during working weeks. However, many accountants work as financial directors or financial advisors to businesses and are often closely involved in the overall running of businesses. A Big Four worldwide firm of accountants and consultants provides a wide range of financial services, including audits, tax advice, insolvencies, assistance on acquisitions and disposals, combining into a whole range of financial and advisory services sometimes involving considerable worldwide travel. They frequently acquire substantial business and industry knowledge, particularly if they specialised, like I did, in the worldwide media and entertainment industry.

As a chartered accountant in the 1980s and 1990s, as mentioned elsewhere in this book, I was the head of KPMG's UK, European and Worldwide media and entertainment-industry practice in the accounting and consulting firm. This involved, by some distance, the largest number of industry clients in number and value throughout the UK, Europe and worldwide in the television, film, radio and music industries. KPMG would be publicly named as signatories on audit reports published with companies' annual accounts but would often not be publicly named on advisory roles for a range of numerous other financial services provided privately to clients, like tax advice, acquisitions, consulting and advisory work. Some of this work would sometimes be carried out by other financial firms rather than the company's auditors. In addition, also as mentioned elsewhere, KPMG were annual exhibitors in the Palais in Cannes, in the south of France, for four film, television and music worldwide industry events each year, for a decade, as well as numerous other industry events in the UK and worldwide. This gleaned a large amount of key information on what was going on in the media and entertainment industry, worldwide.

Consequently, in addition to annual audits, KPMG were often employed by clients to provide a range of other financial services, including advice and consulting on taxation, forecasts, acquisitions and disposals. At the time, I led the KPMG team that had built up a worldwide share of nearly thirty per cent, by value, of financial services provided by accountants, tax advisors and financial consultants to UK, European and Worldwide television and other media companies, as recorded individually in a separate chapter of this book.

It was natural, therefore, that, when there was a big industry story developing in the UK and/or in the worldwide media industry of television, film, radio and publishing, television broadcasters and journalists would contact me as the chairman and head of KPMG's media and entertainment practice for the UK, Europe and worldwide. They were seeking information and asking me to comment for their broadcasting or publishing purposes. They often wanted me to confirm, deny or provide information on the status and backgrounds of large industry transactions, developments and likely outcomes. Journalists often required an independent confirmation in order to verify their stories before publication, and I could often provide this but only when I knew I was not breaching confidentiality issues with clients.

That led to me being quoted and saying numerous general quotes live, by me, in television appearances and in national newspapers and trade magazines on numerous occasions and appearing, quite often, on nationwide television and radio on programmes, like BBC Newsnight, when I would be as informative as permissible without breaching client confidentiality. I would seek to try to assist the journalists but obviously I often could not always provide some, specific detailed information about the work provided for our numerous clients as this was often confidential, particularly if provided in detail.

My relationships with journalists were friendly within the criteria above and, in most cases, there was considerable mutual respect. I knew the boundaries particularly as I had recruited some former industry journalists and heads of industry trade organisations to work for me as KPMG media and entertainment consultants to the industry. The overall industry knowledge collectively accumulated was considerable and very rare.

The most difficult appearances of numerous broadcasting experiences made over several years were to appear live on numerous annual BBC breakfast and other news programmes whenever topical. For example, for some decades, I commented live and in detail on how well the British Film Industry had fared internationally in all of the categories at the annual Academy Awards. This was far from easy, as this appearance was at 8 am on breakfast television in the UK, which was the same time as midnight the previous evening in Los Angeles where the awards took place. With the time difference of eight hours, I would not know the winners when the car picked me up from my home just before 6 am to take me to the BBC studios, where I would be handed a copy of the winners. Therefore, I, necessarily, had to prepare individual notes of brief comments in advance for every candidate on the short list should they win. This would be reduced to relevant comments when I reached the BBC studios and was notified of the winners, which sometimes were not the favourites predicted by some in advance.

I made some other major television appearances during the several months when there was substantial public and business interest in guessing how many bids would be made and which broadcasters were likely to win the twenty advertised UK regional and national breakfast ITV commercial television franchises. This was when programmers commenced readvertising on 1 January 1993. I obviously knew the several regions where KPMG were acting for the existing franchise holder or, privately, were acting for challengers. This covered a substantial majority of the franchises, including all the large ones, being advertised. No other partner in KPMG could accept an assignment before I had confirmed that it was appropriate to do so and would not lead to potential embarrassment.

On the BBC's Newsnight programme the night before the franchise winners were announced, I stated that the approximate number of new bidders would be about twenty-five, in addition to the sixteen incumbents, and I thought that the number of franchises lost by the incumbent broadcasters would be no more than five. This was based on what I had, in total, gleaned often confidentially and what I anticipated based on industry and private knowledge. The above was very close to when the overall results were eventually announced with forty different bidders for the total number of franchises available.

During the event, four existing franchise holders lost their licences so there was not a huge turmoil in the industry.

I have made several tens of further live television appearances relating to the worldwide media and entertainment industry and other financial issues that were relevant at the time. The secret is to keep comments as brief as possible, to appear as normal as possible and not lose one's temper when an interviewer repeatedly seeks to challenge views to suit their purpose. Sometimes, like a King's Counsel in court, they will repeat questions several times in order to try to get to the opinion they were seeking. However, it was always necessary to stick to what I knew and not disclose specific information, which would breach confidential arrangements and unfairly damage any business in the industry.

I often met and spoke to numerous industry journalists and provided general comments to help them, when appropriate, for public information. I also spoke at numerous industry conferences on issues facing the industry. All that I needed to do was withhold privileged and private information, when appropriate, to respect that journalists were just doing their jobs and stick to the boundaries of my clients' confidential information. I would often, at the journalists' requests, write an article in trade magazines and national newspapers or appear live on television and radio on the then-current issues of general industry significance. This would save journalists time as they did not have to spend so much time themselves.

A further development was when I recruited the head of the Independent Programme and Producers Association and the editor of the weekly *Broadcast* magazine to join our media and entertainment consulting practice. Both of them had accumulated substantial knowledge of the UK television and film industry at that time, and this was immensely valuable to clients of all sizes in the industry, as well as to me and my industry expert staff.

Being an Expert Witness in Court Cases

There are little more strenuous business activities in life than to be chosen as a so-called expert witness in life than to appear as an expert witness in a court case.

Quite often, if the spokesperson for the defendant cannot successfully establish that some or all of the written or oral evidence provided by the prosecution is incorrect, he/she will probably lose the legal case and the client will suffer the consequences. He/she will, therefore, use every option to challenge or attempt to confuse the expert witness in order to seek to prove that his/her evidence is incorrect, unreliable or untrustworthy so as to diminish in whole or in part the potential damage to the defendant. Quite often, the same question will be asked several times seeking a variation of any kind in the witness' tale. It is important to remain clear and demonstrate consistency to avoid any more challenges than absolutely necessary.

One of the main legal cases for me was to act for SMG (the Scottish Media Group) as the defendants in a case brought to court by Chris Evans, the well-known mainly radio broadcaster. In December 1997, shortly after joining Virgin Radio, Chris Evans had bought Virgin Radio from Sir Richard Branson for £83 million. Part of the deal involved Evans signing up as programme presenter to the station on a long-term contract. He then earned an annual salary of £1.7 million. Audience figures were at an all-time high with Evans in charge.

In 2000, Evans sold Virgin Radio together with his television production company, Ginger, to Scottish Media for £225 million. In early 2001, relations between him and Virgin Radio were becoming very difficult, and, in June 2021, he was sacked after failing to turn up for work for five days in a row. He said he was ill, but he was pictured during those days at a local pub with his wife, Billy Piper.

Evans sued Scottish Media for £8.6 million worth of Scottish Media's share options he claimed was owed to him as a result of Virgin Radio's sale. He was counter-sued by Scottish Media for breach of contract.

I was appointed as an expert witness for Scottish Media during several weeks of legal argument in the 2003 court case between legal representatives of Evans and Scottish Media. It is never an easy position to hold as the defendants have to use every available option to challenge your evidence because if they are unsuccessful, they are likely to lose the case, which is what happened. They will often ask very slightly different questions several times, hoping that there will be slightly different responses claiming your evidence is uncertain and should be discarded, which will help their client.

In June 2003, Evans lost his claim, and the judge awarded substantial damages to Scottish Media.

In a second unrelated case, two youngish British men obtained substantial funds from UK finance sources to redevelop a number of properties near Les Champs-Élysées in Paris. A year or so later, all the funds had been drawn down pending planning consents, but none of them were spent on the proposed redevelopments. I acted as an expert witness to demonstrate this misuse of funds.

Keeping in Touch with Former Employees (Sometimes Called Alumni)

All the original Big Eight firms of accountants – reduced to four firms, following mergers – needed to recruit large numbers of mainly university graduates every year so they would spend at least three to four years in training whilst working for the firm. This was competitive with the other large firms. At the end of that period, the graduates would hopefully pass the second of the two examinations needed to qualify as chartered accountants. It could take longer if there were periodic failures leading to retakes several months later. They would work with the firm's already-qualified staff on numerous services, like audits, tax advice, acquisitions and sometimes on insolvencies. The firm also recruited qualified chartered accountants from smaller firms.

Upon qualification a few years later, some of the former graduates would wish to stay in the firm for some more years, seeking further experience and potential promotion in the firm. However, many of them did not wish to stay for a long time and would choose to leave to take up employment with commercial companies, mainly in the UK, but sometimes overseas.

Several would join existing clients of the firm after they had qualified, but others would join other firms. Frequently, they had some allegiance to their former firm where they had trained and qualified with, but the firm they were joining would often already have employed different accountants for various services. Every few years, it was good and normal practice for clients to review the situation and conduct a "beauty parade" of, say, three firms of accountants, with the winner obtaining or keeping the assignment.

It, therefore, became quite important that the firm they qualified with kept in touch with the graduates who had left as they potentially were future clients. It was, therefore, necessary for the firm, for example, to invite them periodically to social functions, solely for reunions with others and to keep them informed of major developments in the firm.

These various reunion functions became a necessity. For example, there is still at least one reunion a year for former partners in KPMG's London office, sponsored by the firm to keep in touch and be in the frame, if professional services are required by the alumni. Some other reunions for former staff still take place.

I headed up the alumni programme for several years, backed up by numerous colleagues in KPMG. It undoubtedly safeguarded and expanded the overall work gained from clients of the firm.

Consequently, things have moved on significantly and are now totally different from the era of some forty years ago when it was deemed unprofessional for professional service companies to advertise their services, like most other companies would do to promote their business. In this book, there are various mentions of external promotions promoting the firm, including, for example, sponsoring men and women golf professionals worldwide to wear KPMG on their hats every time they play in golf tournaments somewhere in the world. Then, those tournaments and events are broadcast, sometimes for many hours, on the worldwide viewers' televisions.

Things have come a long way from when firms' names became more widely known only when professional firms were named for running significant insolvencies, including one of the biggest names, like Rolls Royce, for example. That company's name had to be in the public domain as all subsequent business transactions would involve the insolvency firm named to conduct the business.

Private London Members and Social Clubs

When working in various senior positions for KPMG, whose offices were in Blackfriars in London, there were not many upmarket venues in the vicinity for meeting with clients and buying them a meal when appropriate. Having established KPMG's media and entertainment practice, it was, therefore, a good idea to join two social clubs that were in tune with the industry. There are many social clubs in London, but I have been fortunate to be a member of two private members' clubs; both are very suitable for professionals working in the media and entertainment industries.

The first club I joined as a member was the then-newly established Soho House Club on Greek Street in Soho. This was a great place to meet clients and other people and to have some libation and sometimes a meal. Whilst not huge on each floor, there was always a great atmosphere in the club, and I made several more friends amongst the trendy membership. The annual membership charge was quite reasonable, given the location and the offering. It was also open until 2 am, after most establishments closed at just after 11 pm, and, on occasion, this was useful to conclude business or social discussions. Over the years, the membership gradually increased, and the club later moved to Dean Street, not far away.

Many of my guests had never been there before I took them, and, therefore, they regarded it as a privilege to be invited there.

It was not surprising that The Soho House Club gradually expanded its membership, and it often became very busy at peak times. It also established other Soho House venues around the country.

The second club that also held its attractions was The Hospital Club (later known as the H Club, then closing in 2020, due to the effects of the COVID-19 pandemic) on Endell Street, in Covent

Garden. Overall, the club was spread over seven floors with a nice restaurant and a few bars and lounges. It also had eighteen bedrooms, a TV room and a screening room. Unlike the Soho House Club, a jacket was required.

Whilst not spending too much time in both of the above clubs, I did greatly enjoy some memorable experiences.

Opening Bars and Restaurants

Functions with Famous Performers
During the 1990s, having accumulated a substantial list of worldwide and nationally known media and entertainment-industry clients and relationships for KPMG, details of which are elsewhere in this book, I was gradually appointed as the partner in charge of KPMG's UK, European and Worldwide Media and Entertainment practice. Due to the rapid expansion and accumulation of clients in this practice, I was further appointed as the partner in charge of KPMG's UK, European and Worldwide Marketing. This had separate marketing budgets over and above what KPMG partners spent specifically in their own countries.

Whilst not to my great desire, it was mandated that I should gradually hand over virtually all of my clients, like London Weekend Television and the Rank Film and Television Group, to more junior partners and concentrate on my two worldwide administrative roles. This involved considerable worldwide travelling. However, I kept in periodic contact with many clients through regular meetings at various media and entertainment trade-association functions, including those held by the Royal Television Society, the Radio Academy and BAFTA, and I was made a Fellow in several institutions.

I was quite happy to have some lunches in the partners' dining room when not out with clients but, to have a rest, I acquired leases of the decent-sized City Golf Bar and the City Boardroom situated above that, both just off Ludgate Circus at Blackfriars. Both were a very short distance across the road from KPMG's offices in Puddle Dock and Salisbury Square and from Goldman Sachs' offices on Fleet Street. Lunchtime takings were good, but it was not worth opening the relatively small City Boardroom in the evenings.

To raise the profile of the City Golf Bar, a stage was constructed, and several live bands and professional comedians played on several Thursday evenings with tickets advertised and sold. My favourite group, The Searchers, played there, as did Suzi Quattro and Spandau Ballet. These were unbelievable evenings.

Owning Racehorses

For the first forty years of my life, whilst interested in sport generally, I did not have the time nor the particular interest to follow horseracing and, generally, I do not greatly do so today. I have never been a regular gambler on football pools or racehorses or the many other ways that one can have a bet, hoping to win.

An exception I would make is a regular weekly contribution to the National Lottery. Further, on numerous odd occasions I, like many, have bought sweepstake tickets for local or national charities or good causes or had a small bet on the Grand National. I have never had a bet on any of the horses I owned a share of as this would generally be relatively small compared to the prize money if the horse was well placed in the result, then the horse's value would also increase significantly if successful.

However, whilst chairing KPMG's worldwide music and entertainment industry practice with numerous well-known clients, like Universal, Chrysalis and Virgin, it was also natural to be a regular attendee at the annual Silver Clef Charity Awards Dinner in London. This was a significant event in UK's music industry. Since 1976, the awards have raised over £11 million for the Nordoff-Robbins Music Therapy Foundation and honoured some of the greatest names in the music industry. The charity provides therapy for children suffering from physical or developmental disabilities.

Some key supporters were Willie Robertson and Bob Taylor, principal owners of Robertson Taylor. They were the leading specialist brokers for insuring live venues against unanticipated losses, such as bad weather and the absence of scheduled artists who could not feature due to unexpected circumstances.

Robertson Taylor invariably hired a yacht in France's Cannes harbour for entertaining purposes every year during the January week of Marché International du Disque et de l'Édition Musicale

(MIDEM), one of the biggest music industry business events in the world. As mentioned elsewhere, for some fifteen years, I led the KPMG Worldwide Specialist Music Industry Team with a promotional stand in the Palais building, adjoining the harbour. I was always delighted to be invited every year to the Robertson Taylor boat for lunch on one day as that was where the key international music industry personnel worldwide would be present.

Willie Robertson was very keen on horseracing and suggested that a group of us should collectively buy a bay colt horse called Clef of Silver, including training fees, and contribute all race prize money and the eventual value of the horse to the Nordoff-Robbins Music Therapy Foundation. I was one of several subscribers to this partnership called the Silver Clef Racing Venture, trained by William Jarvis.

Clef of Silver ran twelve times between June 1997 and July 2000. He won two races and finished second four times. It was a really fun experience to be present at some of the racecourses and to see the relevant races live on television and to contribute the winnings to a worthy charity.

Over the years, I had minority share ownerships of seven other horses named the following, together with their total winnings:

Horse Name	£000 Won
Western Roots	18
Mataram	32
Atlantic Affair	41
Swain Bridge	5
Turn Me On	6
Batchelor Affair	2
Churchills Victory	2
Sunhill Dancer	6

However, the horse of greatest significance to me was as follows:

As mentioned elsewhere I had been the external audit partner and financial advisor to the Chrysalis Group, one of the seven largest music companies in the world, for some fifteen years until 2000. This was when I voluntarily left KPMG to take up some of the many job offers I had previously received but, at the time, was not at liberty to take up for potential conflict issues. I was immediately invited to join the Board of the Stock Exchange-listed company, Chrysalis Group plc, which I did as recorded in the Music Industry Chapter in this book.

The chairman and major shareholder of Chrysalis, Chris Wright, owned a significant stud farm for racehorses in Wiltshire. He knew through the music industry that I had a stake in Clef of Silver, and he asked me if I would like to have a 50/50 partnership with him on a horse of his choosing. He was finding it increasingly difficult to name horses as they obviously had to be approved as different from any other racehorses before, and this was never easy. He was very happy with me naming the horse Casa Catalina after the Spanish restaurant I had owned then, in Blackfriars in Central London. He was also happy that Mark Johnston would be the trainer in the very North of England. With his son, Mark has often trained more or, at least, as many winning horses each year as any other trainer and, at the time of this writing, he and his son still have huge successes at all levels of horseracing in the UK.

Casa Catalina won his second race at Thirsk, earning £6,005 up to that date, and Chris, Mark and I thought it was appropriate to then enter him in the forthcoming Goffs Million Race at The Curragh Racecourse in Ireland as Mark thought the horse had a chance of winning the first prize of a million Euros. This is a roll-up race to the extent that, to enter, one needs to pay an initial amount in advance and then a further amount a month later and so on, such that much or all of the million euros prize money would have been paid for by the owners of the horses that run and those who entered originally but had backed out at the various declaration stages.

Mark had engaged a top jockey, Kieron Fallon, to ride Casa Catalina. On race day, I got up at 6 am and flew to Dublin, hired a car and drove to the Curragh in time to meet Mark's wife, Dierdre, for lunch. She said they were cautiously optimistic with Kieron riding, as was the case when we met up with all parties in the parade ring. Kieron mentioned that he planned to be in the first ten to start with, and he aimed to hit the front a furlong out from the finishing line. He did exactly that but, just inside the last furlong, his back leg was stamped on by a horse behind him, and Casa Catalina rose up and lost speed to finish down the field in eighth position. Kieron was furious because, as Casa Catalina was travelling so well, he was convinced he was going to win the race and was decimated for all of us not winning the incredible prize money, including the jockey's and the trainer's usual share of the overall winnings. Needless to say, Chris, Mark, Dierdre and I were also very sad about not achieving what might have been.

Ever since, I never had or wanted to own a significant share of another racehorse nor been a gambler on horses except maybe a couple of pounds occasionally on a punt for a Grand National winner.

However, I have in, recent years, joined the "Owners Group", which purchases horses and then sells the ownership of a horse to numerous individuals. This initially covers the initial purchase cost and a year or two of total outlays on each horse. The individual pays a one-off cost of a few tens of pounds and joins a large number of other subscribers in paying for the cost of the horse, plus all expenses, like training fees, for a defined period of, at least, a year. One can choose horses available based on previous information that is freely and publicly available. Nobody is going to make much money out of this ownership when the share of winnings may be not much more than £10. However, it is a cheap way to have an interest in horse ownership, even though it's small. My latest, from 2021 to 2024, is a small interest in Dutch Decoy, who has been running frequently recently with quite a lot of success. Mark Johnston and his son, Charlie, had trained Dutch Decoy brilliantly up in the very North of England. At the time of writing, Dutch Decoy has already run 43 times, with seven wins, six seconds and five thirds. His total earnings since April 2019 are recorded as £89,437.

Recently, I acquired a very small interest in a horse called Go West, trained by Philip Hobbs in West Somerset, which is just a few miles from where I was brought up. Go West has performed well, up to the time of writing, and has won or been in the first three places in several races. I also acquired a very small interest in Union Island, a horse that Charlie trained.

As time goes by, I may continue to participate with a few tens of pounds to participate further as one takes a keen interest in the outcome, good or bad, at minimal cost.

Significant Auction and Raffles Prizes

Whenever attending a number of charitable events, one is likely to witness that much of the funding obtained for worthy causes comes from raffles for prizes or an auction where attendees bid for items, several of which have been donated and can be significant and original.

Obviously, bidders generally bid only on the items that are of interest to them, and some can be unusual and also can be items of high value. Often, the item will be sold for somewhat less than the market value as there is no cost to the charity with the item having been donated by a supporter.

As in the chapter in this book about leasing hundreds of cars for junior management of what is now KPMG, several suppliers had client entertainment programmes. One of the car suppliers to KPMG was Motorent, who invited my wife and I to its charity event at a top London hotel in support of the company's chosen charity: the Wooden Spoon Society. This charity aids handicapped children who were unlikely unable to walk and were mainly relegated to staying in their specialised home. They, therefore, were always going to be last in any physical activity they experienced and would receive, in metaphoric terms, the "Wooden Spoon".

Motorent held a raffle at this charity event, with tickets that sold for £50 apiece, with the winner of the draw receiving a new Nissan Micra car free of charge. To my wife's and my amazement, we held the winning ticket and won the car. Initially, one of our daughters used it whilst learning to drive and passing her driving test. It was a very useful car for several years after that time.

In 2011, Harrods donated an auction prize, offering unique entrance to their annual sale one hour before it opened to the public. In addition, Harrods gave us access, for a short time the day before their annual bumper sale, so, on the first sale day, we would be quick to confirm the items we wanted to buy before the public had access. We spent several thousands of pounds on items needed, but saved some, too, because everything was bought at the sale prices. It made furnishing a new house a lot easier.

Like many, I have been able to donate a limited sum to numerous charities with good causes and been luckier than most.

Sport Other than Golf

Golf has been the sport I have personally played and loved so much, covering over 60 years of my life. I still do so at the time of writing. There is a separate chapter in this book about playing golf in various countries with numerous people, several whom are or were professionals and/or famous. However, there are several other sports that I have played periodically, sometimes playing well and sometimes less so. I have also been present at some famous events with unique experiences, like the ones immediately below. The unique sport of Nine Pin Skittles, played mainly in annexes to pubs in Somerset, is included in the chapter on Schooling and Early Working Years.

Attending England's 1966 World Cup Victory at Wembley Stadium
An employee in my father's housebuilding business legally applied for and obtained two tickets for the World Cup football final at Wembley in 1966. Due to other commitments later, the employee could not go to the event and offered them to my father, who accepted them. Obviously, at the time of issue, nobody knew who would be playing in the final as the tournament had not even started. Sadly, my father then became ill with a recurrence of malaria arising from his experiences in West Africa during the Second World War.

Upon being offered, my middle brother and I, therefore, gleefully accepted the two tickets and, not surprisingly, we will always remember attending Wembley on that unique occasion with England winning the World Cup.

We were seated level with the edge of the penalty area of the pitch defended by the Germans. With our naked eyes, my brother and I clearly saw the shot from Geoff Hurst bounce over the goal line, as did many spectators around us, including numerous German fans, few of whom doubted the situation.

The referee awarded the goal after a consultation with the linesman who was in a good position to express an opinion. When seeing the television pictures of Geoff Hurst's shot from a camera that was well up the pitch, it proved inconclusive to many, and differences of opinion on whether it was a goal or not have been expressed for many years afterwards.

Football in English League Teams

There are few football league teams from where I originate from, in the West Country of England, with only Plymouth, Exeter, Torquay and the two Bristol teams all forty to sixty miles away from where I was born and lived for the first twenty years of my life. All those teams have achieved relatively little national success for most of my lifetime, although, Bristol City had been in the top division for a short period.

Whilst growing up, I supported my local semi-professional football team of Minehead, originally in the Western League. They fared well as they recruited several semi-professional players from some forty to sixty miles away, in the Bristol area, who had not been retained by the league teams above. Minehead finished in the runners up position in the Western League in 1967 and 1972, under their greatly admired and successful Player Manager, Bob Boyd. They joined the Southern League in 1972, with some success.

In 1978, Minehead lost at Wimbledon by a single goal in the very last minutes of their virtual final league game. In my view and the view of many, including many of the home-team supporters, there was a clear penalty for Minehead later on in the game but the referee did not give it. As a result, Wimbledon finished at the top and were elected to the fourth division of the Football League and rose quickly up the Leagues to the First Division and their FA Cup-winning success in the 1980s.

They have since fallen away. If the referee had given the penalty to Minehead, who knows how things might have been different for both Wimbledon and Minehead? Having beaten Swansea City in the first round of the FA Cup in 1976, Minehead narrowly lost at Portsmouth in the second round in front of a crowd of 14,000. Since then, Minehead have fallen away and, generally, played in local leagues in Somerset. Oh, what might have been!

More significantly nationwide and to the amazement of many, I have been an avid supporter of Newcastle United for nearly seventy years, and many believe that, if I got a cut on my hand, the blood spilt will be black and white, like the Newcastle colours, rather than the usual red blood.

The reason is that, for many early years of my life, the only football matches seen on television were home internationals and the FA Cup final. Newcastle won the Cup only in 1951, 1952 and 1955, when I was very young, and the team had won some playoff games in other years, but they weren't enough to win the Cup in other years. I have gone, with the Toon Army supporters, to many games when they were playing in the South of England. Unbelievably, it is alleged that, at the time of writing, they are the richest football team in the world.

Rugby

Going to a public school at Taunton in my early teenage years, the main sport was rugby not football. I was the "hooker" in the front end of the scrum of my house team at Taunton School. It was bruising, and I was only ever an average player. I did not do this for long!

Whilst on the Board of the Stock Exchange-listed company, Chrysalis plc, Chairman Chris Wright owned the London Wasps rugby team (as well as Queens Park Rangers football team). I attended several matches but that later was reduced to watching the Wasps periodically on television in recent years.

Cricket

I played cricket at Taunton School, and, for some of my late teenage years after I left school at 16, I played for Minehead's second eleven with mixed success.

Snooker

My father was a very keen snooker player, and I will always remember the many games we played together on a table in our home, which was a base for our dining room table. After a while, we had some very competitive games. In later years, I entertained clients of KPMG at Wembley in a box, while watching the annual games at the Masters between snooker legends including Jimmy White and Steve Davis. It was a great opportunity to get to know KPMG's clients better.

Men's Hockey

For a short while after leaving school, I played in goal in local men's hockey matches in the Minehead area. After a relatively short time, I took the safer view of giving up the game.

Tennis

At one of my former homes, there was a tennis court in the garden, and I enjoyed several games with my family and friends.

Long-Distance Car-Trialling and Owning Unusual Cars

My family and I have owned a number of cars over the years, We owned a series of Audis and my beloved no-longer-made Saab cars for several decades. However, I have also owned three other cars that are or have been virtually used only for the purposes of long-distance car-trialling three times a year on weekends in January (South Devon), Easter (North Devon) and October (South Midlands). There are numerous other Motoring Clubs that have their periodic local, mainly one-day events. However, each of my favourite car-trialling events lasted nearly 24 hours. One of the best long car trials in the United Kingdom that still takes place is the Land's End Trial, which first ran long-distance reliability trials in 1901 and has now run, virtually, every year almost continuously since, except during wars, etc.

In April 2024, the 99th annual Land's End Trial of the still originally named Motor Cycling Club took place starting at the competitors' choice from three places in Gloucestershire, Hampshire and Cornwall converging onto a joint starting place in Somerset. The trial included driving throughout the night and finishing seventeen hours later when the last car arrived at Hayle in Cornwall. The normal annual number of 150-160 cars, each one with a mandatory passenger, and some 150 motorcyclists competed.

During the trial, there is at least one compulsory rest/meal stop for one hour. Otherwise, it is continuous driving to one of the fifteen or so special sections off tarmac roads, joining a smallish queue and going up the hill one at a time. Each untarmacked lane or field is virtually one in three steep, and it is often normal, on some muddy and stony sections, for cars to seek better grip by letting the back tyres down to nearer flat to, say, 8/10 psi. These must be pumped up again to nearly 30psi each time at the top of each section as it is illegal to drive on normal roads with lower-than-recommended tyre pressures. Virtually the last section to be climbed on the Land's End Trial is at Blue Hills near Bude in Cornwall, when one drives up a very steep, stony lane on the cliff next to the Bristol Channel. Many hundreds of Easter Saturday holidaymakers come to watch the 150 motorcycles and 150 cars putting great effort into trying to go up the steep hill without stopping, over a six-hour period. This part of the event is very popular with children.

For several years in the 1960s, when I was quite young, I would go to bed in Minehead in Somerset several hours before normal the night before Easter Saturday. I would be woken up to leave home at about 4 am to go with my middle brother and father to watch many of the tail end 300-plus motorbikes and cars 30 miles away trying to get their vehicles up a stony and potholed hill without stopping. This was at one of the early trial sections at Beggars Roost at Lynton in North Devon. On the main A39 road from Minehead, one travels along the beautiful Exmoor Heritage Coast of the Bristol Channel and descends down the very-steep hill to Lynmouth and then up the very steep hill to Lynton, which overlooks Lynmouth. Shortly after, off to the right, there is a further very-steep ancient stony, rutted and muddy untarmacked lane that was used originally by stage coaches and cars before tarmacked roads were constructed. Nowadays, all road vehicles use a tarmacked detour road that increases the distance to the top but does not damage their vehicles.

Beggars Roost was originally named as such because beggars used to live on one of the two banks of the rutted track, knowing that it was so steep and untarmacked and that stage coaches or early year motor vehicles could only go up very slowly. The beggars, therefore, had a chance of running beside the vehicle holding their hands out hoping to receive money, food or gifts donated by the passengers.

Every year since, to date, some spectators stand on the top of the muddy bank at Beggars Roost very early every Easter Saturday morning to watch and often shout to support and encourage the nearby motorcyclists and car drivers and passengers below to get to the top of the section without stopping. Drivers never get out of first gear as attempts to change gear would decelerate the car, and this would rarely be sufficient to avoid the car stopping and would likely lead to failure. Cars have to be manual as automatic cars would be useless. In later years, to make things more difficult, several car classes have had to stop halfway up and, when flagged down, have a few seconds to restart again from a stationary position.

One of my early lifetime adult ambitions was that, when I was old enough, I wanted to drive a car up Beggars Roost without stopping and successfully climb the other fifteen sections before finishing the car trial in Cornwall each Easter Saturday. When my son became old enough, I bought a 1955 Morgan Plus 4 car with the specific purpose of competing annually every year at Easter and the other two other annual car trials with him initially as a passenger.

Some years later, one of my daughters wanted to compete and drive the Morgan, so I purchased a Marlin ready-made Noddy-lookalike-kit car for my son to also compete with his friend on the three annual trials. My daughter and I, therefore, continued to use the Morgan for several years also in the same three events in the first paragraph above.

After several years, I realised that we were damaging the quite valuable Morgan, not necessarily significantly, but the Morgan was always repaired to maintain its significant value as an historic car. It has now been sold at auction for a considerable amount.

My son and his friend continue to compete in all three annual trials, and I purchased a second Marlin kit car for my son-in-law and me to enter the trials until very recent years.

While driving in these trials, one sees spectacular off-road scenery that many normal drivers never witness.

Timeshare Ownerships in United States and in England (Some Good, Others Not So Much)

The very mention of the word *timeshare* sparks a number of different reactions amongst interested owners and many others, for example, like:

- Do I want to go to the same place every year for my holiday for many, many years?
- What happens if there is a clash of dates in a year when I have something else I want to do?
- How do I sell it when I no longer want it?
- Isn't it expensive for what it is, or is it a good value, generally?

I have owned two timeshares with different objectives and values:

1. Orange Lake in Kissimmee, near Orlando, in Florida, for two weeks in August
2. The Langdales in the Lake District in Cumbria, North West England for the last week of July.

My experiences of each long-term opportunities are set out below.

Orange Lake

Charles Kemmons Wilson started Holiday Inns in 1952 and rapidly expanded that group with numerous hotels, initially all over the United States. By 1972, his vision for the group was achieved fully, and he retired from his position as Chairman of Holiday Inns. He moved to Florida, where he gradually built, at Orange Lake in Kissimmee, a very large number of attractive residential properties, which catered to families on a timeshare basis for stays of a week or two each year. This was very close to where the many theme parks and other attractions were already there or were being built, mainly by Disney and Universal Studios but also many other attractions and accommodations.

For our first three-week holiday in the United States, we landed in Florida on a fly-drive holiday. We drove South down to the Mexican border and then, in three weeks, drove the whole way up the Eastern side of the United States up to the Niagara Falls' border with Canada. Basically, after every second day of travelling, we planned to stay two nights instead of one, including a somewhat longer stay at Disney World and all the other holiday attractions in Florida, which expanded rapidly before and after our visit.

Whilst staying in Orlando, we accepted an invitation and spent a little time visiting the Orange Lake Country Club. As the children were quite young, we agreed to purchase weeks thirty-one and thirty-two in August of each year of a two-bedroom property, which included a sofa with a pull-out bed in the living area. The unit easily accommodated five people. We returned five times, gradually in the ensuing years, for at least two weeks each time. We visited Disney's Magic Kingdom, Epcot, Sea World, Universal Studios, Typhoon Lagoon, Cypress Gardens, MGM Studios and many other attractions of a then-rapidly expanding holiday area. Each year, we had to pay a maintenance fee for the property, but our share was just a 26th of the annual figure, for our two weeks. In several years, due to the considerable number of weekly sold units in Orange Lake, the maintenance fee often was not recovered by visitors willing to rent if we did not wish to use it.

The last time we went there was in 2011. The property was rented out in 2013 at a figure below the maintenance fee, and we sold it a couple of years later for a sum less than our purchase price. However, it was a very enjoyable experience, while it lasted, for our children and when our grandchildren were growing up.

The Langdales in North West England

A totally different experience has resulted from our timeshare of week thirty (the last week of July) in the beautiful Langdale Estate in the Windermere countryside in the North West of

England. This is where, for more than 30 years, we have owned a very well-appointed upper floor apartment of a two-storey building in the Lake District for that week every year. If we do not wish to occupy the flat for the week, or offer it to our relatives or friends, it invariably will be let on-site for more than the annual maintenance fee so there is never a negative cash situation in any year. The surrounding area is fantastic for walking to so many different places (assuming it does not rain) and car driving for the odd day or two. Exploring the wider area reveals many stunning views.

In that whole Cumbria area, there are so many quaint villages and safe walks round so many beautiful lakes and hillside areas that, even in July, one often sees relatively few people in many places. It is a real holiday compared to the daily hustle and bustle in the South East of England.

In contrast with Orange Lake, as I believe all the numerous weeks have been sold, our timeshare at The Langdales could be sold at a profit, although this is more likely to be handed down to future generations.

Life as a Head-Hunter

When I voluntarily left KPMG in London in 2000 after 33 years working for them and, in later years, being on the Worldwide Board, I was approached by the highly respected head-hunter, Gillian Carrick. She was a media and entertainment recruitment specialist head-hunter at Goddard Kay Rogers (GKR) in charge of recruiting suitable employees to fulfil vacancies at the high end in UK media and entertainment businesses. She knew that I had become the head of the media and entertainment practice for KPMG in the UK and Worldwide, and I obviously knew a substantial number of executives who worked in that industry as well as many other executives in other industries. She asked me to join her with the intention of assisting her and GKR, generally, to expand the media and entertainment-industry practice.

In the 1990s, a long-awaited corporate report recommended that every one of the Stock Exchange-listed companies should split the role of Chairman and Chief Executive and have at least three non-Executive Directors.

High-end recruitment agencies, therefore, had a bonanza period in a confidential, ultra-secretive world of upmarket businesses with full-time employees' salaries, then, starting at £70,000 per annum and non-executive directors at £30,000 for their part time work. The former figure would be much more now.

Several leading head-hunters' London businesses are in plush and luxurious properties in Mayfair and Belgravia. It is necessary for a head-hunter to learn a vast amount about a client's business, its methods of working and its culture before being able to seek or recommend a suitable candidate. Having been the head of KPMG's Worldwide Media and Entertainment Practice, I clearly knew already many of the possible candidates and that they had acquired much of the necessary information required already.

Head-hunters have consistently been in considerable demand with some of them coming from successful careers in business. They hold extensive databases of publicly known information on individuals and employ researchers to comb through the vast quantity of information available and condense it into the relevant amount for each of those who might be a possible candidate for any individual position.

There was a weekly meeting of all the key staff where progress on individual and potential assignments was discussed. When one of the fellow head-hunters was struggling, I was often able to be quite useful across the Board, based on my knowledge of individuals and experiences gained from my extensive KPMG career.

What disappointed me was that often one of the head-hunters was struggling and had sought assistance at the weekly meetings of all the head-hunters. Due to my extensive experience as a KPMG partner, I passed on detailed knowledge of various individuals who I thought might be appropriate as I knew them well from my KPMG career. Several of these individuals were duly appointed to high-value positions, but the bonus earned for the appointment was not paid to me but to the head-hunter of whom I had advised.

After a year, I got bored and left GKR to take up several other appointments, as stated elsewhere in this book.

Working for Property Businesses

Qualifying as a chartered accountant in Somerset at age 21 and then moving to the home counties and working for what is now KPMG and becoming a London, UK, European and Worldwide Board member of that accounting and consulting firm, my involvement in the family's day-to-day business of housebuilding and funeral operations at nearly 200 miles away, in Somerset, was occasional for many years. As a result, in my early years, my involvement in properties was relatively small, but I was always consulted on key decisions. However, throughout my later adult life, I have been involved in numerous other property businesses in various countries in the world in many different guises. Elsewhere in this book are chapters about selling numerous properties and businesses in Dubai as listed in the Overseas Assignments chapter of this book and, when appointed as the receiver and manager of UK shops and housebuilding companies, details are listed in the Insolvencies chapters of this book.

My father was a partner, and, later, the sole family owner, of a housebuilding business in Somerset, and he and my two older brothers were involved on a full-time basis in that business throughout their working lives. Two of my older brother's children also worked for the family business in their later years. For many years, the business employed bricklayers, carpenters, painters, plumbers, etc. and used relatively few subcontractors whilst building houses.

Consequently, since qualifying as a Chartered Accountant locally and then moving to the London area, my involvement in the West Country business was relatively small and was often only advisory when consulted.

However, in 1970, shortly after I qualified as a chartered accountant in Minehead, and after a five-year training contract and moving to London, I was closely involved in a family decision to incorporate a second company dealing with property investments in Somerset. This was separate from the long-established housebuilding and funeral businesses, which were winding down having covered virtually the whole of the working lives of my father and my two brothers. Shareholdings of the investment company were taken up by my parents, my two brothers, me, our spouses and younger family members.

The accumulated undistributed profits of the housebuilding firm were used to accumulate in a separate business with an investment property portfolio to include freehold interests in:

- Houses, mainly quite old
- Flat blocks
- The local HSBC Bank
- A parade of four shops in the centre of town
- The local Woolworths shop
- Two reversionary properties
- Having no tradesmen remaining, substantial property management fees were incurred on the outsourcing of:
- Maintenance
- Refurbishment
- Building compliance
- Repairs
- Fire safety
- Structural surveys
- Architects
- Plumbing
- Electrical
- Heating equipment
- Painters and decorators
- Solicitors
- Accountants
- Carpenters
- Rent reviews

- Estate agents
- Valuers
- Auctioneers
- Reversionary property fees

The costs of these, in total, were considerable, particularly with many of the houses and flats being many decades old by now.

In addition, at the family's request, I dealt with the purchase of a reversionary property, where a resident wished to realise some or all of the value of the property they live in but chose to remain in their property, living rent-free for the rest of their lives. I had personally previously dealt with one reversionary property that I owned, personally, which had had a favourable financial ending.

As well as preparing the draft of the annual accounts derived from the cash books before they were sent for finalisation to a local chartered accountancy firm in Somerset, I was involved in the acquisition of the local HSBC and Woolworths freeholds that were bought and sold several years later through a London auction house. I was consulted on all significant transactions as a non-executive director of the family company but could not spend a lot of time on this due to my London, UK and international responsibilities at KPMG. The day-to-day operations of the regularly reviewed business plan was brilliantly dealt with by my nephew, who was the former manager of the local HSBC Bank. His local knowledge due to that role was invaluable to the whole family, principally to me and my family. Even though I had been living more than 150 miles away from the company's activities, I was always consulted for approval on larger transactions as a non-executive director and brought up to date on any significant movements during the day-to-day activities. From his records, I would get the statutory accounts prepared for audit and taxation purposes and filing at Companies House. It was a brilliant professional relationship, which benefitted all the others in the family.

At a Board meeting in 2010, it was agreed that all the remaining properties and Stock Exchange investments should be sold gradually over the next few years and the net proceeds distributed to the family members. With the exception of one property, this was done to avoid the potential double taxation on a death in the family with estate duty being payable on the value of the shares owned by the deceased and then taxation on dividends when the assets were eventually sold by the company and the proceeds paid out to beneficiaries, some of which were over the normal retirement age.

Separately, with a business partner in London who had architectural and design qualifications, I helped finance the refurbishments of several flats in West London that needed modernisation. This was a profitable venture, but, even though surpluses were made on the sale of the properties, they were not significant enough to justify the time and business risk involved so the venture did not last long.

Mentoring Young Chartered Accountants' Careers

When I voluntarily left my partnership at KPMG International in 2000, after being a member of the UK, European and Worldwide Board for several years, I considered what future part-time occupations I could participate in to stay in touch with and supplement income from my future pensions. Several are included elsewhere in this book.

The Institute of Chartered Accountants in England and Wales, of which I had then been a member for some 40 years, provided a career-mentoring service to their younger members. This mentoring was provided by much older chartered accountants who had already accumulated wider experience during their careers. Often, the candidates held senior roles in their various businesses but were far from certain on how best their careers could progress in the future, either in their then-occupations and/or potentially with other employers. It was often not easy for them to have some useful discussions internally.

Their then-current employers paid for a year's monthly one-to-one consultations with much older chartered accountants each for an hour or so in the hope that the candidates might respect their loyalty and spend longer with them. This resulted in monthly face-to-face discussions reviewing the existing situation and setting short- and medium-term plans to potentially widen their careers. Employers hoped this would help in their career development internally and, by making this gesture, they would want to stay with them maybe longer than otherwise.

For more than the best part of the first decade in this century, I mentored over a dozen chartered accountant candidates. Initially, with each one, it was hugely thought-provoking to consider all the potential desirable issues in their careers and agreeing to the best course of actions planned to achieve them. The candidates found it helpful to formulate plans to achieve this.

At the outset to throughout, there were numerous matters to discuss, including:

- Authentic leadership
- Choosing suitable external training courses
- Developing external business relationships
- Recruiting and developing high-performing support teams
- Developing and performing a commercial mindset
- Developing adaptive thinking and problem-solving
- Ensuring making time available for team development
- Creating better articulation throughout their organisations
- Developing a flexible adaptive style of thinking with clear messages
- Listening to the significant and relevant views of others
- Developing and using strong messages where necessary.

However, after a year or so, this became less useful as the candidates were usually complying with the plan that was producing the desired results. Therefore, other than encouraging the candidates to keep on track with their plans, there was very little extra one could add as the main objective was already being achieved.

My lasting memory is of mentoring several very bright and personable chartered accountants, and I also learned quite a bit from them about what was going on in the world.

Index

Advertising
Alumni
Bacal Construction
BAFTA
British Broadcasting Company
Car trials
Cannes Film Festival
Charities
Chris Wright, CBE
Chrysalis Group
City Golf Bar
Comedians
Comic Relief
CTBF
Douglas Flint, Sir
Dubai
Expert Witness
Film industry
George Martin, Sir
Golf
Granada Television
Hambros Bank
Head-Hunter
Henry Ansbacher Bank
Hong Kong
IPPA
Japan
Jersey
KPMG

Kuwait
Leasing
London Weekend Television
Mentoring
Middle East
Minehead
Minns and Cranes Music
National Film and Television School
National Westminster Bank
NBC Television
Newspaper industry
N. M. Rothschild
Observer, The
PACT
Phil Mickelson
Pink Floyd
Product placement
Racehorses
Radio Academy
Radio industry
Rank Organisation
Richard Branson, Sir
Rolling Stones
Ronan Rafferty
Royal Television Society
Royal Family
Saudi Arabia
Scottish Media Group

Sport
Sudan
Taunton School
Television industry
Timeshares
Today Newspaper, The

Bank of Middle East
Variety Golf Society
Virgin Group
Wembley
Wooden Spoon Society
Yorkshire Television

The author

David Murrell FCA was born in Minehead, Somerset, in 1946. He was educated at Taunton School between 1956 and 1961, passing sufficient O'levels to train to be a local Chartered Accountant. He passed the necessary examinations to qualify and soon after he joined what is now KPMG in their London office in 1964. He was appointed a London office partner in 1981. He subsequently joined the worldwide board of KPMG and later became chairman of both the Worldwide Media and Entertainment Practice and Worldwide Marketing. In 2000, he left KPMG and joined the board of the Stock Exchange listed Chrysalis Music and Television Group and the Cinema and Television Benelovent Fund and supported other numerous charities. Murrell is a keen golfer, and has played in numerous continents, and continues to be a racehorse owner. His book shows how he became one of the best-known Chartered Accountants in the worldwide Media and Entertainment industry.

novum PUBLISHER FOR NEW AUTHORS

The publisher

He who stops getting better stops being good.

This is the motto of novum publishing, and our focus is on finding new manuscripts, publishing them and offering long-term support to the authors.
Our publishing house was founded in 1997, and since then it has become THE expert for new authors and has won numerous awards.

Our editorial team will peruse each manuscript within a few weeks free of charge and without obligation.

You will find more information about
novum publishing and our books on the internet:

w w w . n o v u m - p u b l i s h i n g . c o . u k